Creating
THE
Inspired House

Creating
THE
Inspired House

Discovering Your Place Called Home

JOHN CONNELL

The Taunton Press

To every homeowner willing to express their true self, to every architect willing to listen, and to every artisan inspired by their vision. Exceptional design is the offspring of exceptional people.

The Taunton Press
Inspiration for hands-on living®

The Taunton Press, Inc., 63 South Main Street, PO Box 5506, Newtown, CT 06470-5506
e-mail: tp@taunton.com
Distributed by Publishers Group West

Editors: Scott Gibson, Peter Chapman
Interior design and layout: Jeannet Leendertse
Illustrator: Chuck Lockhart
Photographer: Rob Karosis

Library of Congress Cataloging-in-Publication Data
Connell, John, 1951-
   Creating the inspired house : discovering your place called home / John Connell.
      p. cm.
   ISBN 1-56158-691-9
   1. Architecture, Domestic--United States. 2. Architecture--United States--20th century. 3.
Architecture--Psychological aspects. 4. Architecture--Human factors. I. Title.
   NA7208.C593 2004
 _ 728'.37--dc22

                                    2004009711
Printed in the United States of America
10 9 8 7 6 5 4 3 2 1

The following manufacturers/names appearing in *Creating the Inspired House* are trademarks:
Game Boy®, Ikea®, Pay-Per-View®, Solatubes®, Syndecrete®

Acknowledgments

Consider the odds. Publisher Jim Childs and television producer Fred Schneider hatched the initial Inspired House concept over four years ago. The reason I got involved was that the notion resonated with my work at the Yestermorrow Design/Build school in Vermont. After a number of lively discussions at The Taunton Press, a new magazine was launched *(Inspired House)* and now a book. What serendipity!

In working on this book, I was lucky enough to collaborate with a whole constellation of talented Taunton people. Chuck Miller, Kevin Ireton, and Marc Vassallo culled through hundreds of potential houses, selecting this seminal first batch of inspired houses. In doing so they helped articulate what defines an "inspired house." Creative director Paula Schlosser, who was at every one of these early meetings, transformed those interminable hours of architectural and thematic discourse into a bright and compelling book design. She also brought in Rob Karosis, whose mouth-watering photography brings space, light, and textured detail to every page. More than just a talented shutterbug, Rob's reassuring ease with the people who graciously allowed us to photograph their homes and his grasp of the book's subtleties made him indispensable to the success of this book.

It's hard for mere words to compete with Rob's fabulous images and Jeannet Leendertse's seamless layout. As a middling writer, I took great comfort from editor-in-chief Maria Taylor's encouragement to write in a fresh heartfelt voice and from Jim Child's belief that this should be a different sort of Taunton book. Still, no one writes a Taunton book alone. In this I had the endlessly patient support of editors Scott Gibson and Peter Chapman, stalwart deep-hitters from the Taunton bench. It would not be an exaggeration to say they co-wrote this book, and I'm honored to have worked with them.

Jim, Maria, Paula, Rob, Scott, and Peter are very busy characters, invariably in meetings and often working "on the road." So am I. The feasibility of this project rests with a handful of more constant individuals who organize the meetings, relay the messages, make the connections, and retrieve what's fallen through the cracks. Deepest thanks to Joanne Bisson, Robyn Doyon-Aitken, Jennifer Renjilian Morris, Irina Woelfle, and Allison Hollett for their invaluable contributions to this project.

Finally, as with any all-consuming project, it is those who keep the home fires banked that deserve the biggest toast. Here's to you my April!

Contents

Introduction

Traditionally, books and magazines about home design depend on dramatic photographs of houses and their interiors while the text explains what the reader is looking at. Besides describing the materials, features, and finishes, the better publications outline underlying design principles, such as proportion, lighting, color, and style. But few, if any, devote much attention to the human drama that goes along with the making of a house.

I hope that *Creating the Inspired House* will be the first of many new house books that include people and their interaction as an integral part of the design story. Here, readers will find that personality, lifestyle, and human values are essential fuel for good design. These have always been key ingredients in residential architecture, but they are rarely explored in books and magazines that focus on distinctive homes.

Of course, the stories in this book lean heavily on beautiful photographs as well. But rather than treat finished houses as inanimate artwork, I've gone behind the scenes to learn how homeowners and professionals have collaborated to produce these remarkable homes. This book holds up these houses not so they can be imitated in size, shape, or materials but rather to demonstrate how inspiration shared by everyone involved can lead to outstanding results.

Where that inspiration comes from is the other intriguing dimension of this book. Each homeowner followed a unique path. Some were dealing with unexpected changes in their lives. Others became committed to the idea of making an expressive and lasting home, while many were simply seduced by the beauty of a particular neighborhood or piece of land. In every case, the motivation was personal.

The personal aspect of "inspiration" and "home" is what makes this book challenging. These are ephemeral qualities that can't be photographed, sourced, or purchased. There are no universal definitions. Rather, these notions evolve in each of us as we make our way through life. An inspired house is the ultimate evidence of that evolution. I hope you will take some delight in the 21 house stories that follow, as well as enjoy the photographs. But don't mistake choices that someone else made about window design or furniture for your own inspiration. These are stories of individual conviction and team vision. They all began with homeowners asking themselves how and where they wanted to live.

Creating your own inspired house begins at home.

The shape and quality of the best houses are born of the care, commitment, and personalities of the people involved.

Houses Are about People

A house for who we are. Wick and Angela St. John realized their life-long dream of raising a family in the country with a lean, contemporary design inspired by a chicken coop.

As sure as birds fly and fish swim, people will always make houses. Even as new houses seem to grow more and more alike, the act of creating a personally significant place in the world still defines the human condition. It's what we do. More than simply a means of survival, our homes and gardens can afford us the opportunity for reflection and self-expression. Where we choose to settle, how and what we build, and how our homes feel when they are finished are all reflections of who we are.

I've been an architect and builder for more than 20 years. Along the way, I've spoken to so many homeowners, interviewed so many architects, and guzzled coffee with so many builders that I no longer see houses merely as objects. For me, what makes some houses remarkable are the animated personalities legible in their design and craftsmanship. The shape and quality of the best houses—I call them inspired houses—are born of the care, commitment, and personalities of the people involved.

So why is it that some houses sparkle with a dramatic human quality while others, even very expensive ones, are barely more than bland? I think it's because it takes a rare blend of ingredients to create an inspired house. Yet under the right conditions, a homeowner's inspiration, an architect's vision, and a builder's craft can come together to produce something that's truly spectacular. There is no sure formula. In some of the chapters that follow, the homeowner is also the designer, or even both builder and designer. Some of these houses are for young parents, others for retired grandparents. Many are new construction, but more are renovations, remodels, or rebuilds. Some are built with family and friends, while others were the products of professional designers and teams of artisans. And, of course, the budgets range all over the place. But there is one common theme: a desire for self-expression and the need to be involved in the process.

Behind most inspired houses lie some entertaining stories, and often a few good lessons. In the 21 houses that make up this book, the bounty is particularly rich. These are not the usual accounts of budget blowouts and weather delays, but tales of inspiration, imagination, and clever problem solving. Above all, these stories are populated with memorable characters caught up in the discovery of a place they call home.

Something More than Shelter

As vital as our homes are to a meaningful existence, the complexity of modern construction has endangered the notion that average people can fashion their own. With rare exceptions, today's custom homes are created by a team of professional designers and builders. Depending on circumstances, this group may include an architect, landscape architect, interior designer, decorator, general contractor, carpenters, plumbers, electricians, as well as other artisans and trades. The challenge associated with keeping all these players moving in the same direction is formidable. Like orchestra musicians or actors in a play, each has a unique contribution to make that is only fully realized when everyone works around a central theme or vision. When this theme reflects the homeowner's dreams and the vision is tailored to the specifics of the site, the resulting house can be truly marvelous.

Occasionally, the right homeowner in the right situation will inspire a well-chosen troupe of professionals to create something far beyond simple shelter. These rare residences are more than just nice houses or trendy designs. Imbued with unique character, these inspired houses are signature expressions of that place called home. Like memorable people, these houses stand out from the crowd. Though by no means extreme in their design, these houses give you the immediate sense that things have been carefully configured

Imbued with unique character, inspired houses are signature expressions of that place called home.

to create a particular result. There is an obvious coherence in the design, not only in the building but also in its adjoining outdoor spaces. There's a style of living evident in the layout and a personality in the décor. In fact, after visiting a truly inspired house, you might get the feeling that you know the homeowners even though you've never met them.

Although there has never been a shortage of interesting people, interesting houses remain comparatively rare. Making even a bland house has become a daunting notion for today's homeowner, so creating an exceptional, personally expressive house is even more improbable. When you come across one, you know it and you can be just as certain of finding great stories in its making.

Though much alike in most ways, each of us is individualized by our walk, our dress, and many other personal mannerisms. So think of the following chapters as the architectural equivalent of people-watching, a chance to explore how the personalities involved can make some houses become memorable. Though we all need houses for basic shelter, each is distinguished by the characters who inspire and create it.

Discovering the Inspired House

What, then, are the ingredients for an inspired house? As I listened to the stories behind these homes, five recurring themes were sounded by their owners, designers, and builders. While not every theme is evident in every house, the first three are almost universal.

A timeless place in nature. By building just below the ridge that first attracted them to the site, John Caner and George Beier were able to preserve it as a place to walk, relax, and take in the view.

Expression of Self

These houses, first and foremost, are an expression of the homeowners' dreams, desires, and lifestyles. Just as important is what the homeowners learn about themselves through their relationships with designers and builders. In fact, the process of designing and building a home precipitates questions about values, lifestyle, and preferences that might never have surfaced otherwise. There are few things that reveal us for who we really are as unequivocally as making a house.

Artful Teamwork

Residential architecture is a team art form. Personal chemistry and creative style can make or break the endeavor. If the designer hears and appreciates what the homeowner is requesting, and if the homeowner is open to what the designer brings to the project, then sparks will fly. When builder, architect, and homeowner pursue the same vision, the whole becomes larger than the sum of its individual parts. In these projects, I discovered a rare collaboration that bordered on choreography. It was artful teamwork.

Memorable Place

The ineffable quality of a memorable place cannot be captured with photos and text alone. You take in these places with more than just your eyes, as if you were reading someone's body language. These houses have a character that is more than the configuration of walls, roof, windows, and

doors. They are fully interwoven with their sites, and they invariably feel as if they've been there for a very long time. Each of the new buildings in this book has used extraordinary means to evoke a sense of permanence. Honoring the neighborhood's architectural context, using historic styles and recycled building parts, and creating careful landscape designs are just a few of the more successful techniques.

Inspired Design

It's time to deflate the myth that good design is just a matter of paying the high fees of big-name architects. Residential design is not like a car wash where you pay at the beginning, get dragged through, and are transformed at the end, touch free. It's more interactive. The houses in this book are unusual for the stories behind them, not for their size, fancy materials, or structural gymnastics. These houses are the results of human need, yearning, collaboration, challenge, and invention; in short, these houses are the results of human drama. Homeowners inspired architects who, in turn, gave shape to their dreams. Builders and artisans turned blueprints into reality. Individually and as a team, everyone left their own imprints on what eventually was the final design.

Ongoing Discovery

Winston Churchill said, "We shape our buildings and thereafter, they shape us." Whatever the ideas for these houses were at first, they were destined to change and evolve. During the creation of an inspired house, everyone involved grows and changes. To solve problems creatively, people must be prepared to look at things in different ways. During construction, a house changes in scale and color. Room sizes and materials are altered. Finally, there is the dramatic transformation of an abstract idea into a built design. Even then, change doesn't stop. The following stories reveal how houses form a link between our innermost lives and the rest of the world, shaping our physical outlook and emotional health, and influencing how we socialize with family and friends. Inspired houses become places where homeowners continue to define who they are and who they will become.

Gathering the Players

Every house in this book began with a homeowner convinced that a certain piece of property had the potential to accommodate their particular vision of home. People with the inspiration and fortitude to make their own house don't just plunk themselves down anywhere. They look for a place with their name on it. Sometimes that means new construction on a virgin lot, more often it means remodeling or even rebuilding an existing structure. (Typically, there are 10 times as many permits issued for renovations as there are for new construction.) Some find their perfect place in the city, some in the country, and most in the suburbs. Despite the differences, the common elements in each of these stories are a homeowner, a location, and a dream.

Although a few of these houses are the inspiration of architect-owners, for the rest, finding the right designer was a threshold decision. Some architects can't understand homeowners' dreams, while others don't even want to hear about them. Then there are architects with signature styles that

lead to one-size-fits-all designs. But there are still plenty of design professionals who are good at listening and even better at reading between the lines. Nothing makes a better story than when an architect, after hearing what the client wants, produces a design that takes the spirit of their requests further than they had imagined it could go. If the chemistry is right and the talent inspired, this is where the core themes for the house will be articulated. Eventually, these ideas are translated into construction documents and then a house. But before that happens, another major player must enter the scene—the builder.

There are few things that reveal us for who we really are as unequivocally as making a house.

Choosing the right contractor is the hardest decision of all since this one professional brings dozens of others along with him. Building a great house requires a constellation of trades, deftly choreographed, and unanimously enamored with the project. These are the minimum conditions for transforming the homeowner's inspiration and the architect's vision into a physically enduring place. During the months it takes to build a house, there are daily opportunities for builders to either safeguard the design or cut corners. It is the contractor or foreman who sets the attitude on site and from whom the other trades take their lead. When the lead builder values the project goals, the crew will follow suit.

In researching this book I've heard many stories of builders augmenting or enhancing some aspect of the project in a way that's completely consistent with the architect's design and the homeowners' wishes. What better proof could there be that all players can share the dreams and themes of the house?

Theater of life. When the Oakland fire took their home, the owners embarked on a rebuilding odyssey led by an unproven design/builder and his crew of young architecture students.

The Story of Your Home

When I graduated from architecture school I was under the misguided impression that people hired architects because of our incredibly innovative ideas. I now understand that most homeowners, if given a chance to freely express themselves, will spin lifestyle visions that make ours look tame. When it comes to personal dreams, needs, and lifestyle, most homeowners need very little help. Trite as it may sound, they only need to believe in themselves.

If there is one idea that this book should discredit, it's the notion that there's a correct way to design your house. The houses featured represent 21 very personal solutions on very specific sites. Each is the result of synergistic collaboration between homeowners, designers, and builders around a clear set of themes. While every owner was concerned about budget, not one mentioned resale value as a central theme. Though they all prized design, none was hunting any style but their own.

The inspirations for these houses are as varied as the people who live in them. The stories are as enthralling as gossip. And the final chapter, in every case, is an expressive house, well sited, beautifully designed, and artfully crafted. It is my fervent hope that in this anthology of house stories readers will find the encouragement to believe in and act on their own personal dreams, and build accordingly.

Simple Pleasures

An economy of moves produced a wealth of life-changing results for Wick and Angela St. John.

Their first step was to leave an in-town Atlanta house for a place in the country. Then it was a matter

of finding the right piece of land and an affordable architect who could understand the kind of house

they wanted to build. They were convinced that a small budget would be adequate as long as they

kept their plans simple and restrained. And if designed with an eye for materials, proportion, and

light, the straightforward little house they had in mind should be beautiful as well as affordable.

Permanent camp site. More than just allowing the appreciation of nature through window views, the design of the gable wall extends the living spaces right out into the landscape. The unusual roof design for the porch lets in plenty of light without overheating the space.

The bare minimum of building. Looking something like the end of a large tent with its flaps open, the design helps to push the structure into the background and emphasize its natural surroundings, a key goal for the owners.

The power of simplicity. Looking like a couple of houses from a Monopoly game, this vernacular composition of straight walls and gable roofs is a masterpiece of architectural design.

Think Small and Simple

When it came to finding the right land and the right architect, Wick and Angela enjoyed supernatural luck. They discovered both almost as soon as they started looking. As a professional landscaper, Wick had worked with many architects, and he knew just how much a good designer could bring to a house. He and Angela agreed that even if they were able to afford no more than a one-room house, setting aside money for an architect would still be worth it.

Bob Cain, an accomplished architect of larger buildings, appreciated his clients' rare attitude. As he listened to them describe a small, simple place on a wooded site, his inner eye conjured forms and patterns taken from the local agrarian tradition he grew up with. The stunning design he produced owes nothing to fancy finishes, expensive materials, or other trendy grandstanding.

Wick had started the process with ideas of his own. He began by sketching a floor plan based on a modern, single-story masonry house he had seen in *Fine Homebuilding* magazine. Immediately familiar with the house, Bob kindly explained that the design would be too expensive, and besides, Wick's draft was drastically premature. Instead, he led the homeowners on a thorough exploration of their 30-acre property to find the best building site. He worked closely with each of them as they developed personal wish lists. And all along the way, he presented numerous design alternatives that might fit their needs as well as their budget.

Their individual wish lists, to no one's surprise, showed a happy amount of overlap. Beyond an open design, both Angela and Wick were keen on wood, stone, natural light, porches, and a fireplace. The overarching inspiration was to create a place suffused with nature far away from the city. Wick told Bob that his ideal house would let him track the sun and the horizon in every season and at all times of the day.

Family favorite. Even on a cloudy day, the bright yellow panel syncopated with the steady beat of the white rafter ends creates a lively ambiance on the front porch. Inviting rather than formal, this entryway attracts people from inside and out to linger in the reliable pleasures of a place in the country.

HEART OF A DESIGN

"I extract the design from the character of the local buildings," says architect Bob Cain. There is a simple, surprisingly contemporary elegance in the agrarian buildings found in this part of the world. Using that palette of materials and forms guarantees that a new building won't stick out, which is exactly the effect that Wick and Angela St. John were hoping to achieve. Wick's careful attention to landscaping also helped. Choosing the site carefully, leaving most of the trees alone, and working around features that were already there all contribute to the sense that the house has been here a long time.

No surprising the cook. From the kitchen island, Angela can see down the glazed bridge, through the entry foyer, and all the way out to where cars arrive beyond the gardens. She also has an easy view of the children playing in the backyard.

Materials, Not Moldings

When carefully chosen materials are brought together without moldings or other fussy detailing, their inherent beauty is highlighted. Humble masonry block, framing lumber, and rough-hewn stone come together in the living room to create an almost Japanese-like tranquility. There is an architectural honesty in such unadorned simplicity.

Control central. Located in the middle of the house, the kitchen is connected with everything inside and out. Angela can socialize with adults and supervise children even as she prepares the meal that will bring them all together.

An Economy of Moves

The final design could easily be mistaken for a couple of renovated chicken coops. At first glance, only the beautiful gardens and a brilliant yellow panel at the entry suggest that this is more than a typical rural renovation. The house consists of two parallel buildings, one longer than the other, bridged by a windowed walkway. The view from the entry, centered in the first of the two buildings, leads straight down the bridge, through the kitchen,a and out the back door to a lush, wooded glade. Glass, wood, and view are everywhere. Standing at the kitchen counter, Angela easily surveys everything from arriving guests to kids playing in the backyard. This feature was one of the top priorities on her wish list.

The larger of the two buildings is organized around a self-contained box, or "module," immediately behind the kitchen. With its own doors, windows, roof and skylights, this module is a sort of house within a house that contains bathrooms, laundry, storage, and mechanical systems. The module appears to float independently within the walls and roof of the larger building around it, as it organizes the house into distinctly public and private zones. On one side of the module are the living and dining spaces and kitchen; on the other side, at the far end of the building, is the master bedroom. The overall effect is light years away from any chicken-coop renovation.

House within a House

Modularity makes it manageable. The 2-ft. module that organizes everything in the design is most easily seen in the shelves running along the outside walls back to the master bedroom.

A box within a box. Containing all the mechanicals, bathrooms, laundry, and storage, the central inside box, or module, also organizes the rest of the house into private and public zones. Natural light enters the box through skylights aligned with those in the outer roof.

19

66 The best thing about floor-to-ceiling windows is that they allow me to keep tabs on my kids when they're playing outside," says Angela St. John, "But they like them, too. When they're inside, they can always see outside. In fact, the first thing our children do when visiting another house is try to pull back the drapes and look out of the windows. 99

Poetry of placement. Simply by aligning the top shelf, the back of the bench, and the door glazing, the fewest number of pieces generate the largest visual effect. This horizontal reference line continues in the proportioning of the screens on the porch.

The sublime power of this design comes from Bob's deft use of a modular structural system. Always simple, never flamboyant, the entire house is organized around an economical 2-ft. grid that accommodates the dimensions of most manufactured building materials. The result is a reliable, neutral framework into which he has inserted windows, doors, and fixtures. Like arranging flowers in a vase, if the placement is skillful there is no need for a fancy container to compete with the intrinsic beauty of the flowers. Bob skipped the trendy design gymnastics, preferring to simply let the materials bring out the best in each other.

Bob's suggested color scheme, never really discussed in advance, came as a mild shock to Angela and Wick. Brilliant yellow for the front door? Characteristically seeking the simple, trend-proof look, Angela and Wick decided to look at some alternative colors. They applied their choices to three large pieces of plywood and placed them one at a time by the front door. Once again, they were amazed at Bob's design sense. While they definitely preferred their colors when viewed on the paint charts, none could compare with the yellow at the larger scale of a house.

A Place Discovered

After 12 years of childless marriage, Angela and Wick had planned a snug little house for two. But just as the footings were being poured, Angela discovered she was pregnant. Plans, of course, had to change, and in the process they learned that a truly inspired house could change right along with them. What would have been Wick's office was transformed into a nursery. Then, a few years later, the guest room suffered a similar fate when a second child was born. With a family of four instead of two, Wick and Angela once again turned to Bob. The addition he produced, while never intended, looks as if it had been part of the plan all along.

These days, when not managing the household from her kitchen, Angela's favorite place is the bedroom porch. On the rare winter mornings when she isn't up with the kids, she loves watching the early morning light move through the bare trees and into the house. For Wick, the fireplace is his favorite winter spot. "Just five minutes in front of the fire," he says, "and I feel totally revived." But unanimity arrives with summer. The entire family agrees that the front porch is the finest place on earth. Many a lazy summer evening finds Wick and Angela relaxing in the glow of the gardens, their plans for both a family and a simple life in the country finally at full fruition.

Proportioning for people. An intermediate divider on screen walls runs just below the top of the chair backs, dividing and protecting the screen while allowing an unobstructed view of the surrounding woodland.

Adding on. Inspired houses are built to accommodate change. This addition came about when a family of two became a family of four.

Hot-Rodding a Fifties Colonial

Jan and Matthew Bryant revived their decrepit 1950s Colonial the way energetic

teenagers might hot-rod an old car. After buying the house in a foreclosure sale, they focused their

initial work on the basics—patching holes in the walls, fixing broken windows, solving a water prob-

lem in the basement, and updating the dysfunctional boiler. But as they addressed these purely practi-

cal concerns, Jan and Matthew came to appreciate the logic in the H-shaped floor plan, the vintage

kitchen layout, and the consistency of hot-water heat. Once they realized how much thought had

gone into subtle aspects of the original design, they decided to find an architect who could help guide

them through some adventurous remodeling.

Subtle design moves revealed. The Bryants lived in their house
for almost a year before they realized that the angled island in the
kitchen aligned perfectly with the pool in the backyard.

An Unusual Collaboration

Matthew hired Matt Schoenherr on intuition and trust even though he was not yet a fully licensed architect. Just getting his career off the ground, Schoenherr asked for a fee befitting a moonlighting intern, but Matthew dismissed it as too little. He suggested paying more and insisted that in return he receive only Matt's best work. And that's what he got. In great measure, that act of faith is what sparked an inspired collaboration that not only got them through the renovation but also continues to this day.

Yet the architect's first efforts fell flat. After making several fruitless presentations for traditionally styled alterations, Schoenherr finally showed Jan and Matthew a book on modern architecture. Bingo. Thereafter, all design proposals were cast in a modern style, which suited Schoenherr as well as the Bryants.

A dedicated student of architecture, Matthew watched every step of the process carefully, constantly asking questions and pushing Schoenherr to explain and expand his design ideas. The relatively simple task of finding a way to protect the entry from ice and snow, for example, soon ballooned into an in-depth exploration of an attached greenhouse. In the end, the greenhouse idea was dropped, but the process of examining it was what really counted. That, in fact, characterized how these two worked together. Matthew and Schoenherr would explore a design problem from every angle before Matthew finally drove the process back down to

Suitable for New England winters. Cleanly detailed stonework along with exposed structure overhead gives this entry a solid, protective feel.

Design keeps it classic. Proportion, materials, and detailing wed this contemporary entry porch to the faux Colonial without denigrating its 1950s features. Stone veneer, a traditional material, helps to bridge the gap between the house and the very modern components of the entry roof.

A '50s floor plan with all the frills. The addition of a floral studio (at far right) and patio renew this 1950s Colonial, giving it fresh vitality and complementing rather than challenging its H-shaped floor plan.

BREAKTHROUGH AT THE ENTRY

In designing a new roof over the entry, architect Matt Schoenherr started with a simple arch, a detail that has its roots in Colonial architecture. Here, the feature proved visually disappointing and oddly uninspiring. The design breakthrough came when Schoenherr rotated the eaves of the new roof slightly forward, creating a curve in plan as well as in elevation. Static as a simple arch, the roof now seems to reach outward, offering the greatest protection at the door and a welcome for visitors. And with the sides of the roof receding toward the house, Schoenherr has introduced a sense of motion that enlivens the front of the house.

Architectural jazz. This eclectic weave of several architectural styles works beautifully. An eye for color, proportion, and materials brings disparate elements together like a smooth jazz improvisation.

Inspired By

This Idea Followed Him Home

Matthew gets deeply involved in the construction details of all the design projects the Bryants work on. Seated in a California restaurant, he became enamored with a billowing canvas canopy shading the patrons. He sketched the basic design on the back of a napkin. When he got home, he teamed up with his local handyman to work out details for a similar awning at the back of the house. Both movable and durable, it's a perfect match for New England weather.

the simplest solution. Not every architect would see this practice as either satisfying or efficient, but Schoenherr enjoyed generating alternative designs as much as Matthew did suggesting them.

Addition Times Four

The Bryants began by converting a mudroom to a flower studio for Jan. Then, preserving the essential core of the house, successive design adventures led to the redesign of the front entry, a new garage, and a pool cabana with pergola.

The overarching design philosophy treated the original house as a host for these thoroughly contemporary additions. The new and surprising juxtapositions are all in keeping with the building's previous contradictions in style. The original exterior, for instance, is faux Colonial even though the house has an open floor plan and what was, at least in the 1950s, a state-of-the-art kitchen. A Colonial-style staircase and balcony co-exist with a living room that looks like something in a timber-frame ski lodge. This same eclectic living room now opens onto a Mediterranean-style patio inspired by a restaurant Matthew visited in Pasadena, California. Because the styles are skillfully executed, this wild combination of styles actually highlights the best aspects of each.

Recycling historic design favorites. This flawless replica of a Colonial staircase leads proudly to a balcony design more suited to a Tyrolean chalet, one of several combinations of different architectural styles in the house. No single theme is allowed to dominate.

Colorful conversion. Formerly a mudroom, Jan's new floral studio with its contemporary curves and colors was an early harbinger of the modern-styled additions that would follow.

Material magic. The sheer mass of stone lends dignity to a factory-built front door. Surrounded by clapboards, the same entry would look as though it were trying to pass for an authentic Colonial feature.

The new front entry replaces a dog-eared doorway, with no protective roof or overhang, which dumped foul weather and ruffled visitors gracelessly into the living room. Schoenherr's protected porch design provides a pause for entering guests. This addition uses the same materials—copper, cedar, and metal—that are found in other new parts of the house. Yet it was Matthew who suggested the stone veneer, which plays an important role in balancing the steel and other modern materials of the entry roof with the more conventional materials used on the rest of the exterior. Without it, the entry would have looked like artificial appliqué.

An innovative, pie-shaped shed represents a high point for collaboration between Schoenherr and his clients. The copper-clad front stands up like a building façade from an old western movie, concealing the cantilevered roof wings requested by Matthew for bikes and outside storage. It's hard to tell who takes more delight in this tiny piece of architecture, the professional or the homeowners.

Personalizing Little Projects

After 26 years of marriage, Jan and Matthew seemed impervious to the interpersonal stress typically experienced by couples involved in a renovation. On the contrary, it reinforced their compatibility. So it wasn't timidity that prevented them from making sweeping structural changes to the original house. Although many other owners would have been tempted to meddle with the 1950s interior, even gut it completely, Jan and Matthew saw value in what they had. They deeply appreciate the vintage kitchen and bathrooms, rejoicing in so small a find as a matching plastic lens for the no-longer-made vanity lights above the sinks. Their enthusiasm for restoring the '50s interior was no less intense than it was for the new additions. Both played a part in an expressive design.

Quality Design Has Staying Power

Kitchen design has evolved since the 1950s, but it's not necessarily better. Every era has produced inspired design, and it's a windfall if you know what to do with it. By analyzing and working with an earlier aesthetic, designers can incorporate modern appliances and conveniences into an older kitchen without sacrificing the coherence of the original design. Details help make this kitchen a jewel. The blender station is an updated version of a fixture that would have been at home in a modern '50s kitchen, and the bread drawer with perforated tin lid dates from even earlier.

Pie shed. Architect and homeowners collaborated on this innovative pie-shaped outbuilding, which was created to meet the growing storage needs of a family with two boys.

A special studio. Collecting, drying, and arranging flowers may well be the origin of Jan's creative design sense. To give her an appropriate studio and have some fun, architect Matt Schoenherr used a large window and a high, skylike ceiling to create a miniature version of the outdoors under roof.

Weaving it all together. The brightly colored window sash and chair rail make a strong counterpoint to the natural wood of the contemporary café chairs and table. Focusing on the vase of flowers or the flower garden outside is a matter of shifting your eyes only slightly, a subliminal effect that blurs the distinction between inside and outside.

Colonial Modern

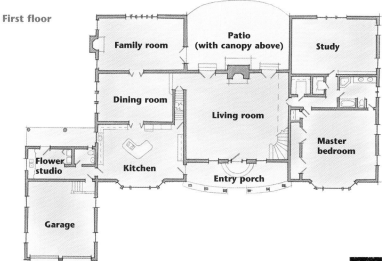

First floor

Family room

Patio (with canopy above)

Study

Dining room

Living room

Flower studio

Kitchen

Master bedroom

Entry porch

Garage

Selfless synergy from inspired collaboration. Matthew wanted a cabana to hide the pool equipment. Not bothered by the pumps, Jan focused on the materials and door design while Schoenherr proposed the pergola and drew it all together.

Schoenherr was stunned when the Bryants bought a lot next door just so they could position the shed exactly where they wanted it. When they ignored traditional resale wisdom, he realized their design inspiration was shaped purely from within. "Pretty much every element in this house is a reflection of us," Matthew says, "either Jan's color sense, style, and decoration or my tendency to push the design shape-wise."

Three years have passed since the sound of hammers energized this site. That's too long for Matthew. He's told Jan he wants to design weather protection for the barbeque, and he wonders whether the attached garage needs further work. Bringing Schoenherr back into the fray, they are now trying to solve the perennial suburban design problem of garage doors that dominate the front of the house. Although various plans for these new design adventures are still preliminary, they even include an engineering study for putting the garage underground.

But there's really no rush. Barbeque shelters are not as urgent as the water they once faced in the basement. It's simply the creative process that's needed. Matthew and Jan will continue to design and redesign parts of their house as long as they feel the urge to express who they are and how they live. "This house has become our artistic expression," says Matthew. "It feels almost as if we wear it."

Urban Innovation

In seaside communities, it's not too surprising to find a boldly modern house in the pageant of styles lining the beach. But the Los Angeles suburb of Venice isn't just any shoreline town, and the home of architects David Hertz and Stacy Fong isn't just any modern house. Certainly the design is beautiful and the spaces are sublime. But the thing that really distinguishes this house is the widespread use of a building material that David invented. The house represents more than the couple's commitment to making a healthy, creative place in the city where they can raise their children. It's also a kind of research-and-development lab in David's quest for greener, more sustainable architecture.

Instead of rooms, tranquility. Even in this unrestrained space, there are well-defined areas to pause for a meal, a book, or a quiet conversation. This kind of design accommodates large groups or intimate gatherings equally.

Doors with duties. The massive garden gate is the equal of any challenge lurking in the city streets. Inside the courtyard, however, entry doors are fashioned from welcoming wood and sized for the age group that might be visiting.

Quiet on the set. In a city neighborhood renowned for cars, it may be nightfall before you get a clear view of the street side of the house.

Signs of Progress

Custom tiles, which can be made in any size and with remarkable accuracy, were among the first and easiest experiments with Syndecrete®, the concretelike synthetic building material invented by David Hertz. Like a talisman for the entire project, these prototype tiles remind Stacy and David that their lifestyle is embossed into the very fabric of the house.

Inspired Prototype

In 1994, when a tiny splinter lot came up for sale in Venice's historic canal district, David and Stacy threw in a lowball bid. What they won was the opportunity to work like dogs for 90 days to nail down financing and win a zoning variance that would allow them to convert a city parking requirement into a courtyard.

Clearly from the "cake-and-eat-it-too school," David envisioned a new kind of urban, family architecture and a showcase for the couple's design practice. The house would also be a live-in R&D project for their company, Syndesis Inc., which David launched in 1983 to market a line of environmentally sensitive building materials. The star product, Syndecrete, is a blend of specially formulated cements and recycled industrial waste that can be cast into almost anything. The Venice house allowed David, an experienced builder, and Stacy, a furniture maker, to test this new material in many applications, including bathtubs, counters, showers, tiles, sinks, and furniture.

When Rooms Aren't Just Four Corners

Materials by themselves, even innovative and very interesting ones, don't guarantee quality architecture. The modern feel of this house comes from David's skillful use of planes and surfaces to define spaces without separating them. Walls start and stop to create a sculpted flow of space rather than traditional room boundaries. In this composition, walls don't contain space so much as organize movement.

This is the thinking behind a wall clad in Syndecrete tiles that starts to the left of the front door, runs all the way to the back of the house, and extends upward through the roof. Because it does so much on so many levels, David calls this the Fanatical Wall. In addition to defining the stairs and organizing traffic flow around the house, this central wall contains the water pipes, waste lines, and electrical cables while also providing the thermal mass needed to maintain even air temperatures. Because the wall eliminates the need for ducts, ceilings can be higher and the flow of space more fluid. What might normally be a simple mechanical wall has been turned into a central design element that establishes architectural themes and spatial relationships throughout the house.

The power of space. Planes and surfaces seem to float and slide in the fluid space of this house. A central "Fanatical Wall" clad with a material invented by the architect anchors the entire design.

Following the Fanatical Wall

As they arrive, guests confront a hint of the Fanatical Wall teamed up with a Syndecrete gate heavy enough to discourage unwelcome intruders. But just inside this formidable entry lies a cozy little courtyard focused on two front doors: a standard size for adults and another, Alice-in-Wonderland size, for children. This whimsical entry opens directly into the social center of the house: kitchen, dining room, a formal fireplace area, and a sunken media den. A central hallway leads to a rear courtyard.

Meals, homework, and art projects take place around the Syndecrete dining table (see the photo on p. 32) or at the polished concrete kitchen counter. Within easy earshot, David and Stacy can sit by the fire, read a book in the den, or work in the office overhanging the area. For those rainy days, protected space in the courtyard shares a large window with the media den. Can life get any better than working on your roller-blade moves while watching MTV?

Modern sidelights. Tempered glass, properly engineered, can support significant loads. This front entry design furthers the impression that the solid planes in this house are supported by the flow of space around them.

View from the courtyard. This view through a window in the den looks all the way through the open first floor to the front door. The den ceiling extends into a bookshelf.

At the top of the stairs, the Fanatical Wall is drenched in sunlight as it runs along one side of a bridge that leads to the kids' bedrooms and bath at the rear of the house. In the front, next to the office, the wall incorporates a final half-flight of stairs leading up to the urbanite's dream bedroom suite. A runway of closets precedes a master bathroom with custom-cast everything, right down to the tiles. In the bedroom, wraparound windows open onto a rooftop playground with sweeping views, a hot tub, fireplace, greenhouse, and even a little driving range. Stacy is passionate about golf, and David's favorite place in the whole house is the sitting area off the bedroom. From this urban eerie, Stacy and David can keep an eye on their family, their house, and their city, enjoying the rooftop vistas without any loss of privacy.

And that's just Phase One.

Growth Means Change

As teenage frenzy inexorably replaces the playgroup shuffle, the family faces a growing need for that rarest of city commodities—space. So when the neighboring lot came on the market, they snapped it up. Just as the first phase was organized around David's central wall, the second and final configuration will be two buildings organized around a central pool courtyard.

Deep space and warm materials. Generous natural light and the use of organic materials soften the cold mass of concrete. The contrast between concrete and wood brings out the best in each.

Half flight up to the master bedroom. Moving up through the house, the Fanatical Wall leads to the master bedroom suite and the rooftop playground.

Like a Polynesian hut. Motivation for getting out of bed includes lounging under the stars, sitting by the fire, or soaking in a hot tub. The wraparound windows and extended roof create the ambiance of an island hut.

Minimal Walls Shape the Flow of Space

This house is held up by the fewest possible walls. In a crowded city, open-ended space is the ultimate luxury, and this design is careful to preserve full front-to-back and side-to-side vistas within two small urban lots. In the soon-to-be-completed second phase, Hertz uses even fewer walls than in the original house and every room enjoys internal views of the courtyard and pool.

Entry

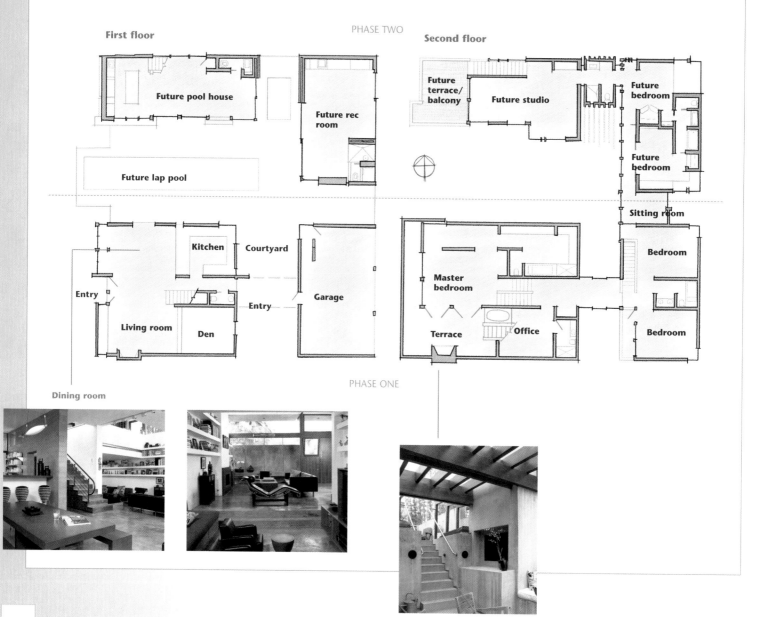

First floor

PHASE TWO

Second floor

Future pool house

Future rec room

Future lap pool

Future terrace/balcony

Future studio

Future bedroom

Future bedroom

Sitting room

Kitchen

Courtyard

Entry

Garage

Entry

Living room

Den

Master bedroom

Bedroom

Terrace

Office

Bedroom

Dining room

PHASE ONE

David credits a trip to Belize for this layout idea but it has just as much to do with family planning. From a big family herself, Stacy believes the best antidote for city temptations is creating better alternatives at home. In their expanded design, all ground-floor rooms will open onto the courtyard. To further blur the boundary between inside and out, walls will be a transparent weave of steel, glass, and ipé—a sustainably harvested rainforest wood. The goal is to create a place where teens have enough breathing space to hang even while adults are socializing not too nearby.

For David and Stacy, innovation will always be the inspiration. Whether it's a better way to raise an urban family or a new process for recycling industrial waste, these architects/inventors/builders will bring creativity and energy to the challenge. Such an exciting atmosphere might even influence the teenagers. Indeed, the most far-reaching consequence of these innovations may well be a new generation of pioneering designers/builders.

Architects do closets. If you allow them to make a closet into art, most architects will design beautiful storage, like this under-stair built-in.

LIVING THROUGH CONSTRUCTION

Construction brings dust, noise, and an inevitable disruption to normal routines. But for architects Stacy Fong and David Hertz, staying put as their house was enlarged seemed natural. David had grown up around construction—he helped his father build Hollywood movie sets and was used to tinkering and inventing—so there was only a little difference between what was on the drawing board and what was being assembled. Construction did not disrupt their lives so much as it validated them: Every dusty day brought them one step closer to the inspired house they had envisioned.

Sleeping Beauty

Sometimes fate plays matchmaker with a house and its owners. Even though Tisha Kalber and Louise Celidonio had previously owned 14 different properties, they would never have predicted they'd end up in the Jamestown, Rhode Island, "ghost house," a harborside derelict whose best days seemed long past. Even before that infamous conflagration, the Mies house was in need of a complete makeover. Built in 1929 on speculation, the Tudor design intended for a flat site was balanced on the hillside like a teenager in her first pair of high heels. The house rose two floors above street level even as the site descended an equal distance to the backyard. While the views were fabulous, there was almost no relationship between the house and the yard. Castle living at its worst.

Harbor beacon. As well as opening the interior to more daylight, the larger windows added by architect Jim Estes also project light like a jack-o'-lantern by night. From some angles along the street, it's possible to see all the way through the house.

Tisha was born in Jamestown, Louise in Boston. Both had grown up along this same New England coastline, so when they began looking for property, they were well familiar with what the region had to offer in the way of housing styles. Indeed, their real estate agent had found them a nice Victorian house, and the owner had accepted their offer. But on their way to sign the sales agreement, Tisha and Louise came upon another house. When they stopped for a look, they discovered that a very odd kind of sale was already underway.

Taking on a Piece of History

The building had been largely boarded up for decades, although its elderly owner still lived there. Although the house was in complete disrepair, it offered one of the finest harbor sites in Jamestown. For one day only, the agent trying to sell the house was allowing prospective buyers 15 minutes apiece to inspect the premises. At the end of the day, the house would go to the highest bidder.

Surprising even themselves, Tisha and Louise got right in line. When they finally gained entry to the cluttered interior, the agent suggested they save some time and simply go up to the third floor. Many stairs later, Tisha and Louise found themselves standing on a box amidst a sea of attic detritus, peering between boards covering a glassless window. The view was life changing.

The ghost house. Every town seems to have a derelict house with overgrown grounds that earns the reputation for being haunted or bewitched. Yet even in disrepair, a grand house collects attention and fans.

With very little discussion, these seasoned property owners continued on to their original destination and asked to be released from their offer for the Victorian. That done, they returned to the harborside house—known locally by a variety of names, including "the dump" and "the ghost house"—and placed an offer. Shortly after noon the following day, they became the new owners, suddenly realizing they had signed themselves up for a massive undertaking. A few inquiries around town revealed that Jim Estes was the only local architect worth considering, so they hired him as precipitously as they had purchased the house. An inspired team was born.

What might have been. The architect's original plan was to tear down the dilapidated house (right) and rebuild (left).

Formerly a musty attic. The view from the third floor was enough to inspire an impulsive purchase and a total remodel. What had been an attic has been transformed into an open kitchen, dining, and living area.

Beach, blanket, and a book. A shoreline cottage that lacks bookshelves is like a sailboat without its sails. This house is missing none of it.

Seeking High Places

At first, Jim wanted to pull down the old hulk and rebuild. "Whatever Jim suggested sounded good to us," remembers Louise. But their new neighbors were obviously less smitten with the plan. Within hours of their intentions leaking out, the neighborhood was abuzz, and by the end of the next day Jim called to announce a new idea. They would keep the building—at least on the outside. There was no point in making enemies before they moved in, and a new structure as high or as close to the water wouldn't meet local building codes anyway.

The house had great views of the harbor, but the interior was dark. "Just give us light," Tisha and Louise told Jim. The plan that followed placed bedrooms on the first floor, with

Nowhere to hang a picture. Inclined walls work well with the Shaker-like interior, but they made it a challenge to build the kitchen. Architect Jim Estes solved the problem by designing an independent island and storage unit that appears parked in the voluminous space like a tugboat waiting at anchor.

the kitchen and living spaces housed in a dramatic double-height space that would take up both the second and third floors. But Tisha and Louise had a few ideas of their own. They had always wanted to live in an upside-down house—a place where rooms typically assigned to the ground-floor level were moved instead to the top of the house—and that's exactly what they had envisioned as they stood that first day in the attic. The clarity of their vision truly inspired Jim. He left behind all of his preconceptions and produced a stunningly personal design.

On the third floor, Jim created an open, airy kitchen, dining, and living area with a pocket porch on the rear of the house. The second floor became a private bedroom suite with a sitting area and plenty of bookshelves. The entry level is all bedrooms and baths for the guests who frequently visit; it's almost like an attached guesthouse. A dumbwaiter takes some of the sting out of all those stairs.

Help with heavy lifting. Estes recommended the installation of this dumbwaiter so it would be easier to move groceries and luggage to upper floors of the house. It also serves as a placeholder for an elevator should the homeowners decide they need one in the future.

Upside-Down House

First floor

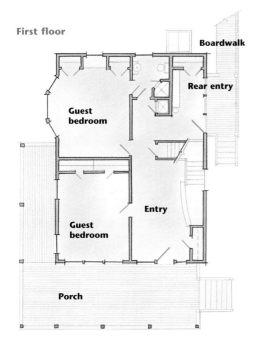

Boardwalk

Rear entry

Guest bedroom

Entry

Guest bedroom

Porch

Second floor

Study

Entry

Hallway

Master bedroom

Third floor

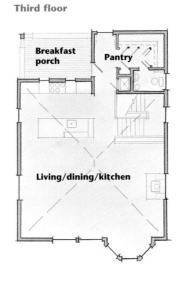

Breakfast porch

Pantry

Living/dining/kitchen

Built-in bounty. The new owners chose built-in clothes storage rather than free-standing furniture for the second-floor bedroom suite, but the room's open, airy feeling compensates for the floor space lost to shelves and built-in cabinets.

More than just a bedroom. With equally stunning views, cozy sitting area, and wraparound bookshelves, the second-floor bedroom is as commodious as the third-floor space, only more private.

Heavenly ascent. Hidden steel allows the stairs to be light and easy to see through. With their easy pitch and hand-finished wood left its natural color, the stairs beckon as they run past the bedroom.

A Good Story

After a couple of remodels, old buildings often end up with a patchwork of woods in the floors. Both the homeowners and their architect struggled with what was the best solution here. It was all but impossible to find matching wood to patch the original floor. But replacing the entire floor would have sanitized the rich character the house had developed over the years. In the end, they decided the varied floor aptly told the story of the house. They plugged, sanded, and finished as best they could. The result is an adventure in different woods, joinery, and levels of craft.

A Lantern on the Harbor

Tisha and Louise share a taste for clean, spare design, neutral colors, and natural materials. They directed Jim toward Shaker, Quaker, and Congregational churches for inspiration. He in turn suggested they look at certain books on seaside cottages. To say they clicked would be an understatement.

Jim left the outside of the house almost entirely original. This preserved the historic pattern and rhythm of buildings along the waterfront street. The only changes were larger windows and a porch cut out of the third floor, both of which were consistently detailed with the rest of the house. The windows fill the rooms with light during the day and transform the house into a huge shoreline lantern by night.

One of two identical structures built around the turn of the 19th century as a rooming house for sailors, the original house was a maze of little rooms. Jim removed so many walls that the building had to be significantly restructured. Jim well knew that the stairs were the key to unifying this design. He produced dozens of sketches, constructed a few scale models, and engaged an engineer to make the stairway as light and transparent as possible. Taken by the beautiful sketches, Louise suggested that all the wood be left natural to highlight the joinery. Subsequently, natural wood with white painted trim became the finish theme.

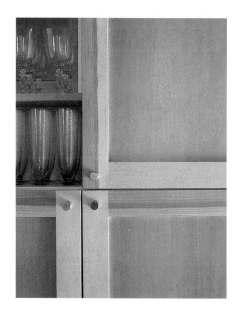

Shaker influence. In contrast to the ornate moldings and trim on the exterior, the new interior is unfussy. Attention to joinery and proportion more than make up for a lack of fancy trim.

Eyes wide open. Comparing the renovated "ghost house" to her twin sister just beyond dramatizes how much larger the windows have become. The windows admit far more light, but the façade is largely unchanged.

No translation necessary. By using traditional white-cedar shingles, white moldings, and double-hung windows, the architect made sure the substantial changes to the building's exterior remained consistent with the pre-existing language of the building.

Homeowner's Journal

Always security conscious, city folk are often surprised by the appeal of a simple porch cantilevered midway between the private and public realms. In the words of Louise Celidonio,

❝ We never imagined we would spend as much time out here as we do. An hour spent on the porch makes you feel like you've been out sailing all day. Everyone, even our guests, sit out here...there's just something about the porch. **❞**

A timber tent. It was a structural trick to open up the third floor all the way to the rafters. A compression ring hidden in the floor keeps the inclined walls from kicking outward.

On the uppermost floor, the entire ceiling is finished in wood, inspired by a fondly remembered bed-and-breakfast they once rented in Aspen. The walls tilt in, reflecting the restored mansard roof. A pocket-size porch overlooks a beautifully planted backyard where Louise has the space to indulge what she calls her "huge gardening needs." Collaborating with landscape designer Martha Moore, she is now working at a scale never possible in her previous houses.

Ongoing Discoveries

Shifting operations from their New York City loft to a three-story weekend and vacation house with a yard takes some adjusting. Tisha, for example, normally would rather go out to eat than cook. Whenever they're in Jamestown, however, she loves to spend the whole day cooking a meal for an evening with friends. It's the first time they've had enough space to entertain more than one or two guests at a time.

Committed bookworms, Louise and Tisha are both surprised to find television creeping into their lives. They put the blame for this cultural concession squarely on Jim Estes' shoulders. The second-floor sanctuary that houses a television is just too comfortable, especially in the evening. With such an incredible view from the upper floors, it's also a little surprising how many hours they spend on the front porch, right next to the sidewalk. But the porch is where they can see their neighbors eye to eye, see the cars roll along, and see the boats tie up. This is where the house becomes a backdrop for village life, and the out-of-towners are appreciated for returning a sleeping beauty to the waking world.

No complaints about the back door. In beach communities, where houses are often crammed together, a side-yard walkway is another way of providing a water view.

A garden sandwich. With house and garage acting as bookends, the perfectly sized garden is a place where Louise can exercise her considerable gardening talents. It's a treat for anyone making their way from car to house.

THESE DAYS, AS THE POPULATION AGES, more and more homeowners are asking for single-level house designs that don't include stairs. But when a narrow lot or steep site makes a multilevel house the best answer, architects and designers have found many ways to make all that climbing between floors more rewarding.

What to do with the space under the stairs is a perennial challenge that has spawned as many creative solutions as there are inventive architects. This tansu-like arrangement of storage cabinets makes great use of the space and is visually appealing.

The experience of using these stairs is enhanced by visual treats along the way, including a wall niche that houses a collection of art objects and views provided by a column of awning windows.

Whimsical details and inventive treatments make this stairway memorable as well as practical for visitors and home-owners alike.

Visual enhancement is often the first response. Treads, railings, balusters, and newel posts all present opportunities for sculptural manipulation. In the hands of an inspired designer, a flight of stairs becomes an interactive art form. Walls that run along the stairs are ideal for art or family photos. The top and bottom of a staircase are among the few places in a house where the designer can be certain of the occupant's orientation, making them perfect places for a special window, niche, or other visual bonus.

A sharply curved stairway might seem too much like the inside of a lighthouse, but the gentle curve of this stair is a comfortable complement to the curved concrete wall and skylight above. Light wood set into the nose of the treads enhances safety.

This oversized landing encourages foot traffic in more than one direction while beckoning visitors with an open approach to the house. It also provides a place to sit.

Stairs are further enriched when they can serve more than one purpose. Treated as a library, gallery, or refuge, a staircase may be sought out for reasons other than going up or down. Children, in particular, seem to understand the appeal of stairways. Halfway between up and down, more than one inspired stair landing with a window seat or sitting area has become a lasting childhood memory.

The Fire Next Time

Like most people, Julia and Will Mies had assumed that the last thing they'd ever need was an architect. But when their house burned to the ground in 1991, they were quickly prompted to hire one. The Mieses contacted Barbara Winslow of the Berkeley, California, firm JSW Architects, setting in motion one of the greatest design collaborations precipitated by the infamous Oakland wildfire.

Even before that conflagration, the house needed a complete makeover. Built on spec in 1929, the faux Tudor had been intended for a flat site. Balanced on the hillside like a backpacker in high heels,

Warmth with or without fire. The arch and inglenook seating added to this seldom-used fireplace provide Julia Mies with a quiet retreat from the bustle of family life without completely isolating her.

Wrong house for the site. The faux Tudor, which was designed for a flat site, perched precariously on the hillside until it was consumed by fire in 1991.

it teetered two floors above street level on a site that descended an equal distance to the backyard. The views were fabulous, but access to the backyard was so awkward that Julia, pregnant when they moved in, avoided it for the first year they lived there. It was castle living at its worst.

A Collaboration Made in Heaven

When Barbara asked the Mieses what they wanted in their new home, they could think of only two features from their old Tudor that were worth re-creating: the fireplace and the views. They asked for a house with an older, classical look, something reminiscent of the California Mission or Mediterranean style. They also requested airy rooms arranged for a casual traffic flow that would give easy access to the front and back yards. Everything that Julia and Will asked for was in keeping with Barbara's own ideas about residential design, making the partnership a rare confluence of interests and outlooks.

Light without sight. The view was great from Julia's kitchen desk until the neighbors rebuilt. The solution was an art glass composition that covers her desk with rosy light while providing its own reliable view.

Prioritize where time is spent. As the owners spend more time sitting than cooking, the informal eating area took the front-row seat to the view. Standing at the stove is still pretty easy on the eyes.

When design means invention. Good designers often have their best inspirations when a situation seems most hopeless. With cabinets and windows competing for limited wall space, morning light was brought into this kitchen by placing glass on the front *and* the back of the cabinets.

Before the fire, Julia and Will had never really thought much about house design. Because they grew up in different parts of the country—Julia in Virginia, Will in Arizona—it would have been no surprise if they'd had very different ideas about what makes an ideal house. But as Barbara explained the choices, it became clear that they both liked the arches, stucco, tile, and low-pitched roofs characteristic of traditional California houses.

At each presentation of Barbara's plans, they became happier and more enthusiastic—the kind of appreciation that's a prime motivator for most architects. Their collaboration ultimately became so compelling for Barbara that she remained actively involved throughout the interior design phase, shopping for tiles and fabrics with the Mieses long after most architects would have called the job done.

Homeowner's Journal

Julia Mies and architect Barbara Winslow treasure some great memories they had while choosing tile for the house. The trick was being able to mix and match different lots to achieve a coherent whole.

" Even though the installer was dubious," says Julia, "we tiled the master bathroom from the manufacturer's 'bone-yard'—where they keep odd lots and seconds. This was a lot cheaper than buying directly from the showroom. *"*

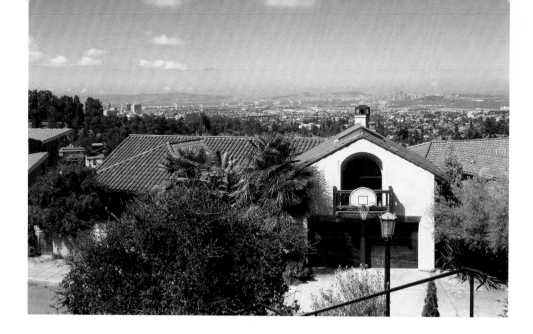

Be a good neighbor. Tall houses in districts crowding the view are the architectural equivalent of standing up in the theater during the best part of the show. Here, a lower street façade expresses community spirit by preserving the neighbor's view.

One-Story Front, Two-Story Back

Main level

Street

Garage (with office above)

Family room

Kitchen

Entry

Living room

Dining room

Inglenook

Breakfast area

Lower level

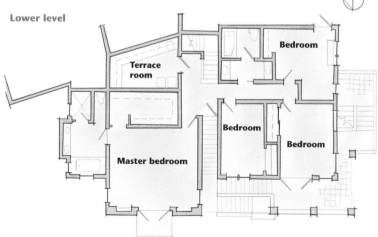

Bedroom

Terrace room

Bedroom

Bedroom

Master bedroom

Creating a Hillside Hacienda

The first and biggest challenge was to arrange the house on the site, and that called for two bold moves. First, the new house would rise only one story from street level with the rest cascading down the precipitous site. Second, the house would be moved as close to the sidewalk as possible. This move would replace the useless front yard with smaller, more intimate courtyards that would relate to the rest of the house.

Julia and Will immediately appreciated the advantages of the proposed layout. Without sacrificing the view, putting the bedrooms on the level below the living spaces meant they would be cooler in summer and warmer in winter. It was also much easier to get to the backyard, making it a place the family could really use, and the house didn't look nearly as imposing from the street.

Treasure the terrain. Challenging sites will imbue buildings with character but only if the design responds to the essential nature of the site. The dramatic pitch of the Oakland hills promotes multi-story designs with great views and playful interiors.

Jump-Start Vintage

One of the easiest ways to ensure a unique look for your house is to incorporate something old or foreign into the design, like this window from India. Stores specializing in architectural salvage—special details from period buildings that have been demolished—are a great place to start, but don't stop there. Antique stores, army-surplus outlets, and even marine suppliers may also provide small but interesting touches. Making sure these found objects are from regions roughly similar in climate or culture keeps them from looking out of place.

The Joy of Discovery

Because the Mieses had come to architecture by accident, they didn't hold their preferences inflexibly. This allowed Barbara to expose them to all sorts of other influences, most of which they embraced enthusiastically.

Eclectic design can be tricky, but Barbara pulled it off by restricting her suggestions on décor to things that would commonly be found in climates similar to Oakland's. Happily coexisting under the overarching Mediterranean style are a window from India, tiles from Tunisia, Craftsman-style light fixtures, and modern metal windows. By its very nature, eclectic décor is warm and welcoming. It suggests that everyone is invited and everything has a place. In reality, everything *doesn't* go with everything. You must either analyze things with a clear head and a sharp eye or, even better, be consistently lucky. Will, for example, found a Chinese ceramic lion that had survived the fire, half buried in the backyard. He set it down by the front door when they were moving into the new house, and today, more than 10 years later, it still looks perfectly at home.

Similar climates produce similar solutions. Although the design is Mediterranean, it is compatible with other hot-climate styles characterized by masonry arches, tile, and terra cotta. The front hall features artifacts from India, Tunisia, and Mexico without upsetting the essentially Mediterranean feel of the house.

Take the High Ground If You Have It

Barbara is convinced that people feel more comfortable when they have views from a high vantage point or from a place that feels protected. With long western views, the numerous decks overlooking the backyard prove how well this theory works in practice—as does the "terrace room," a space just off the stairs halfway between the bedrooms and the backyard. Surrounded by walls on the east but open and covered by a pergola to the west, this outdoor room offers a commanding view of the backyard or a snug refuge in the shade, depending on where you're sitting. Barbara used the same principle in the front-entry foyer, where guests look down and through the sunken living room and take in the views beyond. When the Mieses entertain a crowd, they usually find a clutch of happy guests gathered there.

A fireplace inglenook provides a slightly different kind of refuge. Although seldom used, the fireplace was one of the few things the Mieses missed in their former house. In re-creating it, Barbara added a small sitting area off to the side where Julia can curl up with a book away from household commotion. She can stay in touch with what the rest of the family is up to without being overwhelmed by it.

Not just for dinner parties. Function-specific rooms are costly unless they add something to the adjacent spaces. By opening the dining room to the living room and the hall, all three spaces work together. They each seem larger, and the view is shared by all.

PLACES IN BETWEEN

In a region where the weather is pleasant year-round, places that are neither completely inside nor completely outside have a special appeal. These in-between rooms offer some protection from sun and wind while enhancing and extending the interior layout. Half walled and set under the shade of a pergola, this outdoor room is a refuge from the hubbub of the household as well as a way of getting to the backyard.

Creating a Memorable Place

It's been more than 10 years since the Mieses moved into their new house. Their daughter is now in college, and in a few more years their son will follow. But Julia and Will are not so sure they're interested in designing a new house for their retirement. Sure, there are lots of stairs in their hillside house and Will thinks it might be fun to plan another house, but how could they ever recapture the sense of place? With every passing year, this house on the hill accrues another layer of family history. Even as the children leave and start their own lives, this is the home base to which they will return. After all, memories are one feature even the best architect can't design into a new house.

Set up your views. Besides the obvious long views, most sites have middle views and short views. Inspired houses provide places specifically designed to enjoy the close garden views.

Dinner with a view. One of the great rewards for people willing to build on steep sites is the long view. Whether the long view is of mountains, ocean, city, or plains, the opportunity to stretch one's sight can be deeply restorative.

Remembering a Place

It could easily be mistaken for a summer place on Nantucket or the coast of Maine, but Peter

and Susan Manning's house is a continent away on the southernmost tip of Bainbridge Island in

Washington State. Although Peter modestly calls the style "cozy," it's actually a good deal more. The

warm and welcoming feel of the design comes from skillful remembering and deft re-creation of the

best qualities of their childhood homes.

Three decks in one. The living room extension creates some areas on the deck that are shaded and private while leaving others prominent and sunny. The curved railing gives a nautical feel to the center deck.

Protected arrival. Configuring the house and garage at right angles, along with a bit of landscaping, creates a courtyard fully protected from the weather. A bigger courtyard might accommodate more cars, but it would mean a longer walk to the door.

Susan, an artist and nurse, grew up in New York's Catskill Mountains and along the Delaware River. Peter spent his summers in Maine. After a career in commercial architecture, Peter has gone on to design picturesque, traditionally styled houses. In their own seaside home, the Mannings have deliberately mined the architectural styles of their favorite childhood places, relying on memories of Shingle-style Victorians, Adirondack camps, some funky lighthouses, and even a lifesaving station.

The Pull of the Water

As with all good seaside houses, experiencing this one is a little like taking a stroll to the beach. The closer you get to the water, the stronger its pull becomes. Whether you arrive on foot or by car, you start in a protected courtyard, sheltered by the house and initially out of sight of the water. But moving from courtyard to foyer to living room to oceanside decks, the house continually steps down and opens up, just as the shoreline terrain slopes inevitably to the ocean's edge. As you reach the waterfront side of the house, you step onto a deck running the full length of the first floor with steps to the gardens and, beyond them, the shore. Outside the family room one floor up is another deck with broad views of the water.

Where the land ends. There is a certain compact look to vernacular architecture found along any coast due to the sometimes brutal shoreline weather.

Building by the Beach

The layout for this house was inspired by what Peter Manning calls "a stroll to the water." From an informal entry, guests step down a couple of steps into the living room, down another step out to the deck, and then down a final few steps to the backyard that overlooks the beach just a few steps farther down. If you enter from the garage, a similar "stroll" takes you down to the kitchen and dining room, down to the living room, and so on. Each level change is but a few steps as the circulation meanders through various cozy spaces, each with comfortable seating and stunning views.

Deck

Living room

First floor

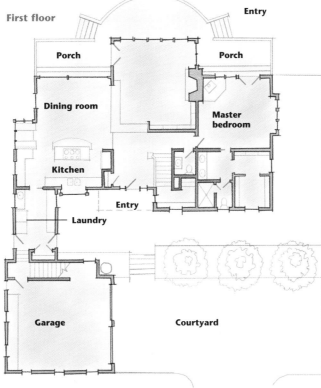

Second floor

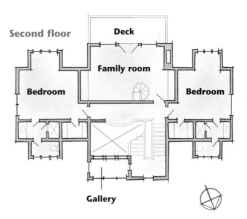

WINDOWS ON THE WORLD

"Light is a major theme of the houses I design," says Peter Manning, "and so by consequence are windows. Capturing the sun, especially here in the Puget Sound region, is critical to our sense of well-being. It is important to design homes so that all important spaces receive abundant natural light. This affects our perception of comfort more than any other aspect of architectural design. But if light is essential, shadow is the complement that gives it power. Relentless and monolithic light is unacceptable."

Open Yet Intimate

The Shingle-style houses and Adirondack camps the Mannings remember are not always small, but they tend to have small rooms and informal interiors that seem comfortable because of an attention to detail. Today's beach-house designs too often incorporate larger spaces than the traditional East Coast structures that inspired Peter and Susan. In this house, public spaces on the first floor are largely open but defined by arched openings and level changes rather than by walls. Combined with oversized windows, spaces that flow into each other create a sense of airy openness. But the Mannings' greatest accomplishment is fearlessly undersizing certain rooms, such as Susan's 100-sq.-ft. studio, while making even relatively larger spaces like the living room seem intimate. By grouping furniture and built-ins, as they've done around the fireplace, they have created cozy zones that seem scaled for individuals or small groups of people.

There are also personal spaces for both Peter and Susan. Susan's rooftop painting and drawing studio is at the highest point of the house. Reached by a spiral stair, it is the ultimate away room whose architectural antecedent might easily be the widow's walk on an old seaside home or even a lighthouse in a small harbor. Peter's space is an office and studio over the garage, where his interests in music, photography, architecture, drawing, and even motorcycling are close at hand.

Cupola studio. At the top of a spiral stair, this 10-ft. by 10-ft. studio never feels cramped because of its 360-degree view, great ventilation, and built-in furniture.

Materials wed house to land. The same local granite used for this Arts and Crafts-style fireplace was used for a masonry skirt along the base of the house.

Warm welcome. This outside room by the front door, open but protected by a roof overhang, creates a warming sense of welcome for visitors even before they walk through the front door.

Echoes of the Shingle Style

The classic Shingle-style entry includes several materials and motifs that recur throughout the house. And so it is with the Mannings' entry, where you first encounter the primary woods for the house—cedar, fir, and cherry—in the front door, its trim, and the surrounding shingles. Doric columns, used at the corner of the garage and then again at the front door, are used repeatedly inside along with another recurring motif, the arch. Stone skirting running around the base of the house is the same granite used in the fireplace. Slate flagstone is used in various sizes in both the kitchen and the bathrooms.

Why get up? The living room accommodates four people, a fireplace, hundreds of books, a television, and a view. That's enough to comfortably wait out any storm.

While the consistent use of similar materials and motifs brings coherence to the house, it shouldn't be seen as an obsession with uniformity. Quite the contrary. By designing a traditional, consistently detailed home, the Mannings have created the perfect container for a personal, eclectic décor. Making places in their house for collectibles, art, and personal treasures is part of what makes it memorable.

Although the house is fundamentally in the Shingle-style tradition, Peter and Susan have included features with entirely different origins. Some are reminiscent of Arts and Crafts bungalows: the combination of brick and stone in the chimney, and detailing on the front door, a corbelled fireplace mantel, the pattern of muntins in the windows.

Be creative with limited materials. Slate used throughout the house helps to unify the design, but cutting different sizes for different areas keeps the look from getting stale.

Office as needed. When the 50-sq.-ft. kitchen island feels overwhelming, the breakfast nook is a cozy refuge. This nook converts to an office with a laptop computer and nearby filing cabinets.

Bathrooms, on the other hand, get some very modern treatments. The kitchen blends traditional cherry cabinetry and state-of-the-art appliances with a layout that's almost commercial. The familiar kitchen island, topped with an expanse of soapstone, serves as a shiplike bridge for the entire house. File cabinets built into the corner by the eating nook and computer wiring allow an office to fold out or in as needed.

This convertible built-in recalls the clever interiors found in fine boats, one of several maritime references throughout the house. In fact, houses in this tradition welcome all maritime metaphors. The bow-shaped upper floor visible as you first enter the house is reflected in the similarly curved deck on the water side. Standing on either is reminiscent of being on the afterdeck of a tall sailing ship. And as a deft finishing touch, the railing posts are topped with glass deck prisms once used to bring light below deck on old ships. Detailing is what holds all these pieces together.

Weaving Family History

Not surprisingly, Peter brings prospective clients home. As they enter, they not only experience the sweep of the first floor but also the two-story space where stairs ascend to the second floor. With a curved balcony and triple-hung windows, it seems to have no additional function beyond housing the stairs. Architecturally, however, it does much more.

In this one space, we are introduced to the materials, the organization, and the spirit of the entire house. Moreover, the ample stairway design accommodates the family photo gallery. Every time they use the stairs, the Mannings are reminded of their extended family and its connection to this house on the water. Inspired houses serve no function more important than the weaving of our past and present into the fabric of an enduring and memorable place.

Light Beacons

Architect Peter Manning is fond of gathering unlikely odds and ends and incorporating them into the houses he designs. Because windows, views, and light played such a central role in the design of this house, he chose glass prisms that once helped light below-deck spaces on sailing ships. Set atop railing posts outside, the prisms are not only an eye-catching detail but also become light beacons at night when lights hidden below are switched on. They also nicely complement the wooden pyramids found throughout the interior detailing.

Think beyond the primary use.
There's nothing wrong or wasteful
in having a grand staircase if it
creates a gallery for family photos.
Many areas in a house do more for
the spirit than they will ever do for
the body.

**Setting up the architectural
experience.** Columns, arches,
pyramids, slate, cherry, and fir:
Almost the entire palette of
motifs and materials is found
within 10 ft. of entering the
front door.

Mansion Moderne

As a successful Chicago real estate developer, Mark Sutherland has seen plenty of unlikely sites transformed into memorable properties with the help of inspired design. So when he won the bid on an odd-sized lot in the historic Wicker Park district, he eagerly designed a modern house that was both visually and technologically unrepressed. He spent a year pitching his modern design to the Commission on Chicago Landmarks. Its review ultimately led to a building with less glass and no rooftop turret, but the spirit of the design is still unabashedly avant-garde. Mark must have won a few fans during the prolonged permit process because the completed house received a city award for its style and use of contemporary materials in a historically compatible design.

Pride of place. Large, unshaded windows collect sunlight in the daytime and give passers-by an unimpeded view of the interior at night. Implicit in this design is an honest openness about the owners' place in the community.

Let the Light In

Klaudia's taste for art and architecture is every bit as progressive as her husband's. She and Mark agree that if they should ever build again, they will have more glass, more light, and wider views. But on this historic street, where adjacent buildings had already established the rhythm and proportioning of windows, they were forced to curb their appetite for floor-to-ceiling glass. Nevertheless, windows are as large as the commission would allow and custom built to get every possible square inch of light.

Even where conventional windows didn't make sense, Mark found ways to admit light. Glass-block walls in a first-floor hall and in the kitchen-level bathroom, for example, face a narrow gangway adjacent to the building next door: It was the light, not the view, that mattered. And in rooms without outside walls, Mark used Solatubes®, a type of skylight that gathers sunlight through a roof-mounted dome

Where privacy is not an issue. A huge glass partition allows the oversized windows to bring the full sweep of the cityscape into bath and bedroom alike. The view from the window at the foot of the tub takes in sidewalks and building fronts along the rest of the block.

Landmark House

Second floor

Terrace

Master bedroom

Bedroom

Walk-in closet

Bedroom

First floor

Entry

Dining room

Deck

Living room

Kitchen

Basement

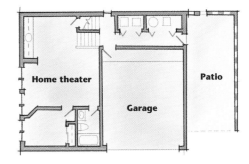

Home theater

Patio

Garage

Light without a switch. Miniature skylight fixtures called Solatubes look just like round ceiling fixtures and supply incredible amounts of free illumination in rooms without windows.

Reflecting a love of light. A full-size mirror and silver paint make the most of the meager sunlight passing through the glass block window in this guest bathroom.

Fitting it all in. Although the building covers the entire site, its appearance is downscaled by a recessed entry and oversized windows. Creative problem solving was still needed to find a place for the garden as well as wall space to hang the art.

and reflects it through a tube to a ceiling-mounted lens. He had a window custom built to give the whirlpool bath a view of the street, and he supersized the glass in the shower stall to get just a little more light into his morning wake-up routine.

Windows take up so much wall space that they occasionally interfered with Mark and Klaudia's equally pressing instinct to find room to hang their art collection. Eventually, a window in the living room was eliminated just to give them a little more wall space. But the question of which piece to hang, as always, is still open for debate.

ARCHITECT'S CORNER

A SETBACK THAT ISN'T

The trick to building a contemporary house in a historic neighborhood is to honor the patterns of existing buildings without actually duplicating their architectural styles. One of the most important patterns in this neighborhood is the relationship of house fronts to the street. On one side, the Sutherlands were bounded by porchless houses built right up to the property line. On the other, houses are set back from the road 12 ft. to accommodate traditional front stairs. Mark split the difference. His contemporary house took a subservient street position with regard to its historic neighbors and at the same time used the setback for a small set of stairs that relate perfectly to houses across the alley. The partial setback leaves enough of the house extending beyond the rest of the houses so that the entire block is visible from the window in the master bedroom whirlpool.

Seeing the Potential

Problem solving, perseverance, and an ability to make hardheaded deals are often the unheralded partners in memorable architectural outcomes. Developer Mark Sutherland saw the potential of this undervalued city lot even though it was small, hemmed in by other buildings, and subject to restrictive historic preservation covenants. He knew he could solve those problems. His resulting design uses high ceilings and large windows to channel light deep into the house with a streetside façade that is at ease in its historic neighborhood. Sensitivity and business savvy allowed Mark to see what many other potential buyers could not.

Inspired by the flowers. Highlighted by their signature stainless steel, blues, and yellows, the Sutherlands' dining room offers a vibrant refuge when inclement weather prevents use of the adjoining deck.

Getting Outside in the City

City living means lots of time inside buildings, and that makes most urbanites yearn for the outdoors. Unfortunately, part of what made this lot affordable was its shallow depth, which ruled out a backyard. Hoping to make do, Mark designed a spacious south-facing deck off the kitchen and dining room. Packed with Klaudia's plants, the deck has proved an ideal spot to enjoy as many meals as weather permits. A rooftop deck, reached by way of an exterior circular stair, is now on the list of possible future projects.

In addition to simply being outside, Klaudia enjoys working the soil and walking the dogs. So, Mark had fruit trees planted at the front of the building between the street and the sidewalk. Hardly a farm, it was all the ground they had. But then the neighboring building came up for sale. Knowing real estate values helped Mark decide to purchase the property and renovate it for upscale rental units. The building became a cash cow, the neighborhood was upgraded, his property values were protected, and, above all, they managed to find space for a garden on part of the lot.

Planted paradise. Klaudia's gardening instincts were originally limited to a walled-in deck, but she nonetheless made good use of the southern exposure. The contrast of the gray concrete blocks makes the colorful flowers all the brighter.

Urban farming. In the city, these little sidewalks running between planting beds and peppered with multicolored shards of granite look right at home.

Surprisingly sophisticated. The Blue Bahia granite hearth might look wild or garish in a less cohesive design, but here it provides a fitting context for the Sutherlands' mostly blue glass-art collection.

Historic Habit, Modern Material

To save money, Mark wanted to use concrete block on the less prominent alley side of the house. A skeptical Landmark Commission pointed out that houses in the neighborhood were built from limestone or common brick laid in simple, traditional patterns. Mark argued that concrete block was the contemporary equivalent of common brick and could, in fact, honor the tradition set by the historic buildings. In time, the commission came around.

Technology Is King

Although Mark hired an architect to help him through the permit process, he proudly claims authorship for the design. Architecturally, he has created spaces with high ceilings, large windows, and finishes that run to polished stone, glass, and stainless steel. As a professional builder, he was able to control costs even while including some of the latest products he found in builder magazines, including composite decking that needs no paint, electric heating coils cast into the sidewalks to melt snow, and manmade stone to replace limestone on the outside of the building.

Although Mark and Klaudia are naturally energetic, they couldn't resist adding some labor-saving touches. The kitchen includes state-of-the-art appliances. On the lowest level of the house, a sophisticated home theater includes a ceiling-mounted projector, automated window shutters, and speakers mounted behind an acoustically transparent screen. A built-in bar poetically conceals the municipal water line as it enters the house.

The nerve center for all these house systems occupies an entire closet opposite the bar. Two computers and several audiovisual components are mounted in a professionally wired rack. Although less visible, these systems are far more pervasive than any of the other innovations. Taking the notion of a "Smart House" to the limit, Mark can control lighting, intercom, television satellite, audio players, heating and cooling, and security from keypads located throughout the house. A wireless touch screen that can be carried any-

Best seat in the house. A television set is an enduring part of the American dream, but the black-and-white box is just a quaint memory compared with the full-featured home theaters of the 21st century.

Everyone's happy but the burglars. Promoted by the city's mayor, such high-tech security gates are approved by the Commission on Chicago's Landmarks. The pointed design alone should dissuade most criminals.

where about the house allows them to control everything from their 400-CD music collection to the garage doors. A closed-circuit camera lets Mark and Klaudia see who's at the front door. If they wish, they can open the door from any keypad, from any phone, or from the wireless touch screen.

Klaudia and Mark are in complete agreement about many parts of the house: its reliance on the latest in technology, its use of modern building materials, its contemporary flavor, even a color scheme that favors yellows and blues. But they like nothing better than a good debate over art and style and how best to blend their sometimes very different tastes. They express themselves freely and look for opportunities to draw guests into discussions over a particular painting or color scheme. It's kept their house, as well as their relationship, lively, interesting, and totally up to date.

Sharing space and view. Just as the kitchen and dining room benefit from the 13-ft.-high volume of the adjoining living room, all three spaces profit from the view and sunlight pouring in through streetside windows.

Transformation for Two

Lynn Hopkins discovered the intimate joys of designing houses almost by chance. After graduating with a degree in architecture, she had gone to work at a big Boston firm that concentrated on commercial architecture. Then Lynn and her husband Ted decided to start a family. When she became pregnant, she cut back her hours at work. With a little time on her hands, Lynn turned her attention to the house that she and Ted had purchased outside the city. It was a pedestrian little Cape in a neighborhood of similar houses, pleasant but unremarkable.

A private space, similar interests. Strict symmetry, simple shapes, and whimsical lights suggest that this could only be a bedroom for two architects. The tranquility that such order creates is perfectly suited to this private room.

Besides removing wallpaper and repainting, the only thing Lynn could initially afford was to rework the entry. It seemed like a tiny alteration. But it was the start of far-reaching changes that would ultimately transform not only the house but also Lynn herself. She had taken the first step toward becoming a residential architect.

Start at the Beginning

Lynn knew the entry to any house is far more than just a door to the inside. An entry is the formal face the house presents to the street. It's a place to pause when coming in from New England weather, somewhere to hang your coat, take off your shoes, and be welcomed. Architecturally, the entry should help visitors get a quick sense of the rest of the house, to understand the layout of rooms and how to get around. A well-designed entry would do all those things, but the one Lynn started with had none of these qualities.

Let the sun shine in. This corner sunroom adds light and elbow room to both the living room and the dining room. Before the advent of open planning, this type of project room was a common way to add flexibility to divided floor plans.

Icon for house and family. The new front door says it all. It's welcoming, protected, and centered, just like the family within.

And so she set to work. On the outside, Lynn created a gabled overhang to protect anyone at the door from the weather. The overhang had obvious practical advantages, and this welcoming roof, the steps leading to the door, and the landscaping around it clearly announce that this is the Front Door. Outside, the redesigned entry was now centered on the house. Inside, the entry rerouted foot traffic from the middle of the living room to the side of the stairs. By relocating the front windows so they were centered on the fireplace, Lynn created a comfortable furniture grouping in front of the hearth. The front of the house suddenly made a lot more sense.

The attention to proportion, detail, and furnishings in this tiny modification made a dramatic improvement in how the house looked and worked. The project convinced Lynn that she could, indeed, correct any of the Cape's shortcomings. Her subsequent renovations, however, required an expanded point of view.

Adjustable view. The reeded glass in these pocket doors admits light into the bedroom without sacrificing privacy.

Preserving Scale and Context

The great strength of the traditional Cape Cod house is its simple proportions. As Lynn's family grew and the need for space became pressing, one of the recurring challenges in residential remodeling presented itself: Where to add on? Too much expansion in any one direction would destroy the essential proportions of the Cape. Moreover, her Harvard schooling had given Lynn a deep respect for context. She refused to blight this delightful neighborhood of postwar Capes with anything that didn't fit in.

Creating comfort. Immediately inside the front door the many layers of this house become apparent, inviting you to enter and make yourself comfortable.

Creating drama with layers. Without giving up any floor space, the addition of this arch creates a sense of entry to a tiny bedroom tucked under the rafters.

The scale of cozy. Oversizing the bay windows in the smaller Cape addition makes it appear even smaller. From the yard, this produces the cozy sensation of a playhouse.

Such limitations might look like an impasse, but for an experienced designer, constraints can actually stimulate creativity. Lynn's solution was to build another, smaller Cape toward the rear of their lot and connect it to the main house with an ell. It's a smaller version of the main house, so it had the effect of visually supporting and enhancing the original. It has the look of a building that grew organically, as many New England structures do, as a family's needs change. More important, the expansion added a much needed master bedroom suite, gave each daughter her own bedroom, and improved the backyard by transforming the patio into a delightful outside room shared by both structures. All the while, the original Cape was left intact.

FITTING IN WITH THE NEIGHBORHOOD

Although it has been substantially reworked and enlarged, Lynn and Ted's house is still recognizably a Cape that blends in easily with its neighbors in this bedroom community outside Boston. "Considering the context of existing houses is especially important in our locale, which has seen its share of teardowns with unfortunate McMansion replacements," Lynn says. "I think my guiding principle was to do something that respected the Capes and the context of this small-scale neighborhood."

Adding a Cape and Ell

First floor

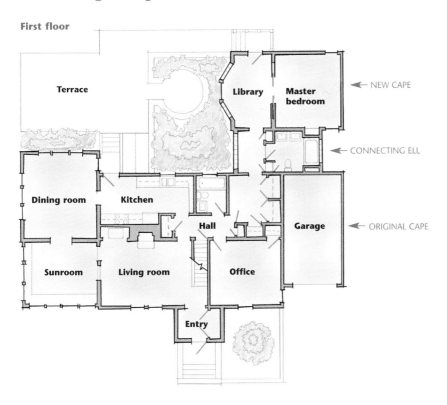

- Terrace
- Library
- Master bedroom ← NEW CAPE
- CONNECTING ELL
- Dining room
- Kitchen
- Garage ← ORIGINAL CAPE
- Hall
- Sunroom
- Living room
- Office
- Entry

Wonderful interior views. In a house of rooms, every door is an opportunity to create an interior vista; each room becomes its own stage set, with opportunities for dramatic entry and framed scenes.

The first shall be last. Remodeling the dining room and creating a patio outside the kitchen were among the owners' first goals. Budget constraints delayed these changes until the end.

83

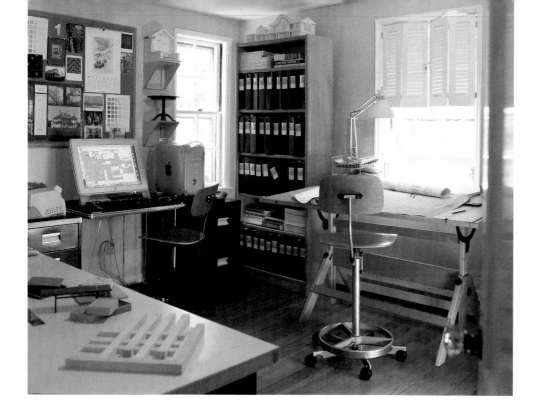

Staffing up.
Although a home office is rarely this neat, when Lynn can't find her design books, she knows to look in the girls' rooms, where they are already considering a bedroom makeover.

It's the Little Things That Count

Keeping the buildings small concentrated Lynn's design attention on the details. What she came to appreciate through these renovations was the importance of detail in maintaining human scale and warmth, concepts that are often forgotten in designing bigger buildings. She had been inspired ever since architecture school by Charles Rennie Mackintosh and other Arts and Crafts designers who understood detailing and ornament. Now she had a chance to try her own hand.

Lynn initially created furniture and casework that was clearly derived from her heroes. Working with her father, an amateur cabinetmaker, she explored the joinery, materials, and finishes that made these designs so compelling. She learned by experimenting. Lynn asked her father to cut pieces of scrap wood into different shapes and proportions and then she played with the pieces, arranging and rearranging them until she had formed clear ideas about interior detailing. It was a grown-up game of blocks that helped Lynn move her own skills forward. As her experience and confidence grew, she created designs that remained appropriate to the Cape Cod origins of her house but were still uniquely hers. Unlike trendy great rooms and soaring cathedral spaces, the interiors that Lynn designed are nicely scaled for people and deliciously detailed.

Details Make the Design

Carefully crafted details are at the heart of the Arts and Crafts style. Brackets, grills, and furniture are all opportunities to introduce eye-pleasing proportion and detailing without resorting to ornamentation that would look out of place. Relying on her cabinetmaker father for raw materials, Lynn experimented with pieces of wood in different sizes and simple shapes, rearranging them until she arrived at a well-proportioned detail that could be translated into trim or furniture.

Any excuse for fine woodworking.
Of course, bookshelves don't need glazed doors, but it's an opportunity to create a handcrafted aesthetic. And it does make buying hardcover books easier to justify.

New Directions

Lynn's husband, Ted, is now a principal in the same firm where they both started. Lynn, however, has embraced a new direction where individual, identifiable people, not the anonymity of massive commercial structures, provide the ultimate design inspiration. And the sophisticated transformation of her little Cape hasn't gone unnoticed in her community. Lynn is now in growing demand as a residential architect, and her skills in that challenging field are improving with each project and every handcrafted detail.

A room for all reasons. Besides giving direct access to the patio, this sitting area in the master bedroom suite is also a reading room where the entire family can gather on lazy mornings and the girls can do their homework.

ONE OF THE MOST TELLING FEATURES of an inspired house is its relationship with the surrounding landscape. Accomplished architects understand that their designs don't stop at the walls or even at the edge of the property. Everything you can see, smell, and hear is part of the experience. This is why the best designs weave these two worlds together in a tapestry of different-sized spaces, some with walls and some without.

The challenge of city living is to retain some feeling for the larger natural world. Potted plants can go a long way, but if the rooftop is available, nothing beats the long view.

Landscape design responds to location. In the constrained landscape of the city, outdoor space is zealously protected, and long views are particularly valued. Rooftop decks, balconies, and pocketbook gardens are common strategies for connecting the urbanite with a larger natural world. In the wide-open country, the situation is reversed. Here, design wants to define and give a sense of place to the landscape associated with the house. Pergolas, walk-

Just as with interior spaces, an outdoor room can be defined by a change in floor treatment or ceiling height. The retractable canvas awning that protects this outdoor room was inspired by a visit to a restaurant.

The design for this Sonoma, California, house grouped rooms into several distinct buildings around a pool, patio, and outdoor kitchen. The arrangement makes outdoor spaces feel integral with interior rooms.

With fences, gardens, steps, and an arbor, this backyard has been transformed into a series of differently scaled spaces organized around a central lawn.

ways, arbors, and hedgerows are but a few of the methods for creating a sense of enclosure. And in the suburbs, fences and shrubs are the "walls that make good neighbors."

Irrespective of location, the treatment of exterior spaces must flow from the core design of the house. At the same time, the hand-in-glove fit achieved by most of these designers is the result of detailed site analysis before making that first drawing.

Almost every room in this Oakland, California, residence looks onto this tiny patio. So compelling is its allure that the owners enjoy most of their meals outside, even in light rain.

A Builder's House

To the surprise of his Ivy League classmates, David Farmer joined a building crew as

soon as he graduated from college. Three decades later, his passion for construction hasn't waned,

even though his desk duties now eclipse his hammer time. When he and his wife, Gay, decided to

buy and remodel an 850-sq.-ft. Spanish-style cottage outside of Denver, he intended to lavish a life-

time of knowledge on the project and spend as much time with hammer in hand as possible.

Interior vistas. The sunroom is the core of the house, with easy
connections to the kitchen, dining room, living area, and master
suite. Arched windows frame interior views and give a sense of
connectedness to everything in the house.

David and Gay succeeded in making this house a true expression of themselves but only after dodging a major pitfall that David often lectures his clients about: namely, changing the design during construction. In this case, close collaboration between the couple, their architect, and others on the project saved the day. And none of it made David waver in his heartfelt belief that there's no better place to put your time and money than your home.

The Good Architect

David's construction firm, Boa Construction, is frequently the choice of high-end clients, many of whom hire architects. Like most builders, David has mixed feelings about this profession. Yet he never misses a chance to champion Jim Mitchell, the architect on this project, as creative, openminded, and able to solve problems without letting his ego get in the way.

David initially gave Jim a few aesthetic guidelines and asked him to prepare floor plans and elevations—just enough to get through the permit application. David figured that he and Gay could fine-tune the interior later. But when "later" finally came, it was Jim who rearranged the floor plan at the last minute and made the interior work.

Old-fashioned neighborhood. Mature trees, ample yards, and varied architectural styles more than make up for the small size of most houses in this neighborhood.

Street identity. More than doubled in size, the house still has the same cottagelike feel from the street. The secret is architect Jim Mitchell's sensitive understanding of proportion and detail along with Gay's upgrade of all the existing plantings.

A jewel in the garden. Seen here from the new patio, the original two-car hacienda-style garage features a constellation of sweet details, including its own outdoor fireplace and intimate sitting area.

Cottage Makeover

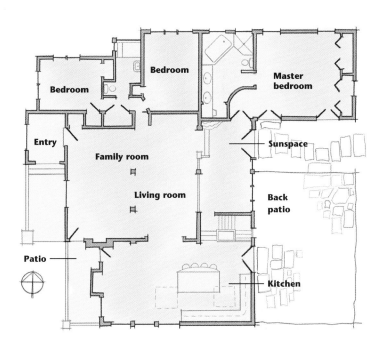

As instructed, Jim's original drawings deftly blended new and old, preserving the architectural scale and detailing on the front of the modest 1932 house while opening the back to a new flagstone patio through a series of double doors and well-placed windows. In all, the square footage would more than double. Jim separated the master suite from other bedrooms in a small wing, accessed through a small sunspace, but preserved important architectural details and left some of the original rooms as they were. The original cottagelike feel of the house survived intact.

> **❝** The kitchen countertop is a piece of Pedra Dorado limestone with a honed, not polished, finish. We were warned about using limestone for a kitchen counter. But this piece was so much more appealing than the typical granite products, we decided to take the risk. Although we have found that lemon juice does slightly etch the surface, normal day-to-day activities seem to buff these etchings right out and it just looks spectacular. **❞**

A few features make it special. Simple factory-built cabinets combined with limestone counters and a broken-edge splash lift this kitchen out of the ordinary. Add Gay's collection of water pitchers and it becomes uniquely personal and expressive.

But with construction well underway, David and Gay were still unhappy with the configuration of the kitchen. They were at a dead end until Carol Mathers, a designer friend, proposed moving the kitchen to an entirely different space than originally intended. This was a *Eureka!* moment. Besides solving problems with kitchen layout, the relocation allowed an expanded sunspace to become the natural center of the house. With one inspired move, everything came together.

Broken-Field Running

Although the floor plan was settled, there were other trials ahead. One of them was the heavy-timber trusses David was trying to design. He built and rejected two versions before he developed one he liked, prompting job foreman Andy Satterthwaite to begin calling the project "House of Many Trusses." When forms for interior arches went through a similar design-by-dumpster process, Andy renamed it "The House of the Rising Costs." David may have gotten a slow start on some of these details, but trial and error is a time-honored tradition among even great architects, and the process fostered a sense that getting it right counted for a lot.

The final fit. Heavy-timber trusses define the kitchen ceiling. Although it took three tries for David to fine-tune the design, the process emphasized the importance of craft.

Every time David comes home he revels in the feeling that the house is a perfect fit for his and Gay's outlook and interests. The trusses, the arches, and the exacting craft that went into the house will all easily outlast the memory of a few extra mortgage payments and a few false steps. One of his biggest joys is looking around at the work and recalling who figured out what, whose hands had made it. "Creating the team," he says, "is the first and often the most important part of the project."

Housing other times and places. This niche was specifically designed to house heirloom family furniture. The candy-striped archway was inspired by a book called *Casa Mexicana.*

Dinner with friends. A mirror collection, furniture from an old family homestead, and roof beams installed by the owner all help to make the house a uniquely personal enclave.

Collections Make Connections

Initially, David and Gay hired an interior designer to help them chose stone, tile, and colors. But Gay's personal collections and family furnishings bring an ambiance unavailable from any store. She sees a house as a balance of "strong opinions" expressed by the people, pets, garden, and extended family that together give it life. Almost every piece of furniture or wall hanging has a story attached to it. Many items come from the family ranch in Walensburg, Colorado, a town with a strong Spanish heritage where Gay grew up. Ask about any piece of art and there is a story, more often about the maker than about the object. It is an eclectic family of things, living happily against Gay's bold Mexican color scheme.

Gay collects mementos, objects with stories. Mounted throughout the house, her collection of mirrors populates and bounces sunlight into all of the spaces. One mirror is elaborate enough to display a whole separate collection of tiny shoes. She found a spot for her collection of water pitchers in the kitchen.

Big bathroom magic. Windows and mirrors make even cramped bathrooms feel expansive. If the window faces a public space, it can be creatively obscured with art glass. Here, the floral theme works perfectly with the Verde marble.

Collections within collections. Gay's many collections animate the house. This mirrored display case, from her mirror collection, actually houses a collection of tiny shoes, a gift from her mother.

Flooring for the ages. Antique southern yellow pine makes a durable, richly colored floor in the bedroom. Resawn from large timbers, the flooring has real character, but David admits it's not for everyone.

Preserving the Best Features

The most memorable parts of this house have been skillfully preserved. A vintage letter-slot/doorbell is the first thing you notice as you stand at the arched front door, made from beautiful plywood back when plywood was more wood than glue. All interior door hardware has been salvaged from the existing house. The original fireplace has been preserved, made even more prominent when David raised the ceilings. The master bedroom-turned-office has been preserved in its entirety, as have many of the arch-topped casement windows.

Then there are the stories that come with an old house. Originally built as workers' housing, this cottage once sheltered a family of four boys (that's not much more than 140 sq. ft. per person). Even at its increased size, the house seems to overflow with life. Paintings, furniture, collections, pets, and plants inhabit the spaces, filling them with ongoing stories.

David still reminds his clients that a house is about enjoying life, not making an investment. "You wouldn't hear them asking what the return on investment is on their summer vacation or that $300 dinner they had last night. So why do they think of their homes that way?" A house becomes a home when it's about the satisfaction people experience from living in it. And David now understands the tendency of clients to change their minds during construction. He realizes that it doesn't make the project any cheaper. But it always makes it better.

UP REALLY CLOSE

The Cans Go Here

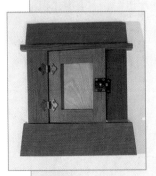

Gay convinced the job foreman to make this beer-can recycling chute as a surprise. The trim has the same happy-go-lucky spirit as the primitive brickwork around the fireplace and floats on the wall in the neighborhood of a couple of equally eccentric light switches. Not only does the chute operate flawlessly, sending empties right to a recycling bin, but it also helps to remind David and Gay that life is fun.

Learning to relax. In an effort to slow down, David bought an easy chair and set up a comfortable corner for reading. The original fireplace and arched windows create a relaxed ambiance with a sense of history.

When craft was cheap. This beautiful arched-top casement window might easily be found in one of today's budget-busting mansions, but it's a rare find in this tiny working-class cottage from the 1930s.

Designing with an Eraser

Like an architectural geode, this house is as stunningly beautiful on the inside as it is utterly

unremarkable on the outside. Hiding a spare Japanese aesthetic inside this 1960s tract house is only

the first of many inspired ideas to emerge from Roberta Hanson and Frank Sciannella's collaboration

with architect Mark McInturff.

Taught by her engineer father as a child to look at houses and see more than the obvious, Roberta

is no stranger to design. She habitually studies the work of local architects in magazines and at design

shows, and when she and Frank decided it was time for a renovation, they interviewed six architect

Tag-team tasting. With two people cooking at once, a kitchen
needs to be both commodious and well laid out. In addition to
being efficient, this sunny kitchen has equal access to the deck and
dining room and is a real hub of household activity.

Diamond in the rough. A geode looks like any other rock until you break it open and so does this everyday subdivision ranch. Its stunning interior radiates color and light.

Knowing When to Go Against the Grain

In a design that is everywhere straight and rectangular, the deft placement of one circular element can be stunning. This Japanese-inspired round window transforms an everyday kitchenscape into a Mondrian-like kaleidoscope. With a set of shelves on one side of the wall and a work of art on the other, this beautiful composition changes with the day's light and the viewer's position. Inspired design is often a case of small moves delivering big effects.

Recurring rail. Every room has a door onto a deck that runs the entire length of the house and overlooks a park adjoining the backyard. The pipe railing mirrors the railing near the front entry, a recurring theme that helps unite inside and outside spaces.

candidates. McInturff was the only one to suggest that they *not* build an addition. Subtraction, in fact, would be the key. "We can design this project with an eraser," he told them.

Staying Put

Roberta and Frank had lived in Rockville, Maryland, for six years and expected to retire in a few more. Instead of planning to build another house for retirement, they had resolved to stay put. But without modifications, they told Mark, the house just wouldn't work for them. Roberta had long wanted to remodel the kitchen, and Frank was equally unhappy with the master bathroom.

Mark doesn't use elaborate questionnaires or psychological profiles to understand his clients' needs. Rather, he sketches up various design proposals and then measures his clients' reactions to them. After a few sketch sessions with Mark, Roberta and Frank were enthralled with the possibilities.

Mark showed them a few preliminary designs involving only the removal of existing walls. Seeing the potential, they quickly became more articulate, describing their former home in California with its bright interiors and easy accessibility to

Consistency heightens impact. Horizontal glass surfaces are clear, glass installed vertically is etched, and walls are mostly white—a consistent system that makes color and displayed objects all the more apparent.

the outdoors. They also divulged their appreciation for Japanese design and glass art and their practice of cooking in tandem. Besides changes to the kitchen and bathroom, other specifics included a big dining-room table and enough storage for Roberta's sizable culinary library.

As he sketched out responses to their growing list of requests, Mark realized these homeowners were willing to push the process, to really have fun. The increasingly enjoyable collaboration quickly gained momentum.

Deep diagonals at the entry. Removing all but the essential walls opens up a view deep into the interior or all the way through to the exterior.

Designed for Light, Not for Sale

Real estate agents prefer houses with a living room, dining room, study, library, and as many bedrooms and bathrooms as possible. Before today's ever-larger "starter castles" became popular, developers created many-roomed houses by keeping the rooms tiny. Such rabbit warrens were easy to sell but terrible to live in. Mark realized immediately that the house would be dramatically improved by allowing more light inside. And that meant putting it on an architectural diet, erasing what it didn't need.

He removed walls between the living room, the dining room, and the study and enlarged the master bedroom suite. And to bring light into the now open floor plan, Mark added glass doors and floor-to-ceiling windows along a new deck— long and ocean-liner-like—that faced a park. Voila! Bay Area ambiance in a '60s suburban ranch.

And the Walls Came Down

Before

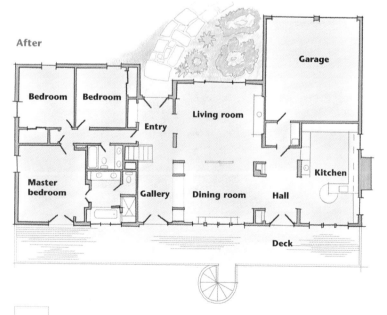

After

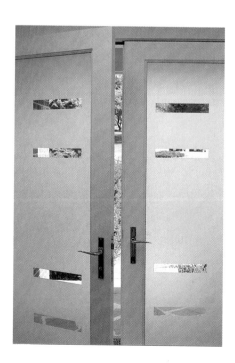

New door in the neighborhood. House-tour guests, deliverymen, and even Halloween trick-or-treaters remark on these formal but friendly etched-glass doors. Quite an improvement over the original door, which had three little windows on a diagonal.

Glass on glass. Endlessly varied, glass can be colored, clear, or etched. It's the ultimate architectural surface, allowing the eye to ride along the edge, pause on the face, or see clear through.

Well-tempered table setting. The strength of steel allows the supports for this table to be exquisitely thin. Remarkably, the tempered glass, at ¾ in. thick, is almost as strong.

Frank and Roberta enjoy watching people's first reactions. When the double front doors open, guests are usually transfixed. The living, dining, and gallery areas are layered spaces that flow one into another, never completely enclosed. A palette of black granite, thick glass, and white maple produces a flowing, museumlike openness. Mark likes to have at least one unbroken line of sight that extends all the way through his designs. This house has several. And those are only the big moves.

Japanese-Like Subtlety

Throughout the house, Mark's innovations with glass give interior spaces a feeling of buoyancy. A round kitchen table seems to float from a corner of the cabinets, supported from below by slender steel rails. A glass sideboard hovers just inside the window wall facing the rear deck. And Roberta's perfectly lit glass collection seems suspended in space on trimless glass shelves.

WORKING WITH GLASS

Asked to open the interior of a dark 1960s ranch to more light, architect Mark McInturff used glass for much more than new windows. Etched panels of glass between the dining room and living room create the sense of separate rooms without blocking light. Elsewhere, glass finds its way into the dining room table, a dining room sideboard cantilevered from a window mullion, and a table in the kitchen. Glass lends a Japanese-like minimalism and sculptural quality to the house with an architectural vocabulary all its own.

The first hint of the Japanese influence on design is apparent at the front doors of etched glass. There is also the teahouse window in the kitchen that has been aligned with a matching mirror at the end of the hall and a diaphanous glass panel between them. The floor-to-ceiling panel mimics the effects of a thin, fabric scrim, allowing light to pass freely between living room and dining room without connecting them into one oversized space. Best of all is the solution for the perennial face-off between television and fireplace hearth. Above the fireplace of black granite, the television is housed in a white maple cabinet with miniature barn doors that ride on red cantilevered tracks. Initially, Frank was not thrilled with this design until Mark explained that it would resemble a kimono when the doors were open. Now Frank delights in showing it off to visitors.

And then there are the colors. With the project largely finished, the walls languished in white primer until the architect traveled to Italy. When he returned, colors harvested in Tuscany were used to accentuate the layered surfaces and shape the flow of space. Choices on exactly which colors to use often waited until Mark and project architect Peter Noonan stood before the blank walls. But one thing

Better than a wall. Glass can do everything a wall does and more. These fixed-glass panes define the dining area, contain the activity, create interest, and transmit light. You could even hang a picture on them.

Kimono cabinet. Here's an ingenious solution for the cohabitation of modern multimedia with the traditional fireplace. This clever cabinetry opens to become a media center in the shape of a kimono, but it doesn't obscure the elegant hearth when the door is closed.

It Was a Sign!

The success of a design, even from a very good architect, is never assured until the homeowners have moved in. A few bright harbingers never hurt. "It was late October and we were moving out of the basement, the project finally complete," remembers Frank. "As I came to the top of the stairs, the early morning light was coming in horizontally through the living room windows, illuminating everything in the house all the way to the back dining room wall. It was like a sign!"

The Zen of baking. Roberta, the family baker, created this pastry station to make maximum use of the granite counters. The lowered section is for kneading and rolling dough.

they were certain of was that color should be applied to one face of the display cabinets rather than wrap around corners to adjacent walls. This crisp treatment keeps color two-dimensional while beautifully emphasizing the sculptural qualities of the glass objects housed inside.

Too Much Fun to Stop

While Mark was off studying Italian colors, Frank and Roberta were happily hunting contemporary furnishings, paintings, and glass throughout the Washington, D.C., area and beyond. They knew what they wanted, waiting almost a year for one piece to be made in Vermont. Mark now sends his other clients to the same stores.

Frank and Roberta lived in the basement during construction, an arrangement that no doubt seemed trying at times. Now, closer than ever to retirement, they miss both the excitement of the project and their satisfying collaboration with Mark. The feeling must be mutual since he's agreed to work with them on their basement renovation, a job he would normally pass over as too small. Roberta smiles when she's asked about this upcoming second phase of their renovation. She and Frank can always use the additional bedrooms when their grandchildren visit. "But," she adds, "I think it's more because we've discovered that design is just what we like to do."

Hard-working colors. With cool colors on one side and warm colors on the other, the three room dividers create entirely different effects depending on which way you're facing. The colors are very carefully matched to the furnishings, giving the overall space a sumptuous coherence from any angle.

Tip Top House

Like a welcoming beacon, the three-story tower bids a stately welcome as you round the last

bend in the drive and approach Tip Top House. If you have found this Tuscan-like enclave in the

hills of Sonoma, California, it's likely you're a guest, one of the many who give the house its main

reason for being. John Caner and George Beier created this getaway as a gathering place, wedding

their love for family and friends with a devotion to this dramatic landscape.

Guest tower. A three-story tower visually dominates the site, especially
on the approach to the house. With an open viewing area on the top
floor that overlooks a lap pool and courtyard, the tower also houses a
study and ground-floor quarters for guests.

Discreet design makes a good neighbor. Huddled just off the top of the knoll, the house enjoys the view without being seen from the valley floor. The layout follows the topography of the hillside.

Even as they are hosts to their guests, John and George consider themselves guests on the land. The reasons for building this house may have been driven by human needs, but its architecture derives clearly from the landscape. Four earthen structures, perfectly scaled and sewn into the terrain, make visitors feel as if they've happened upon a very old complex of farm buildings far in the country.

The Right People

When John and George came across this piece of land, they were instantly swept away. Realizing that it was an extraordinary place to build, the pair interviewed more than a dozen architects for the project. Strolling to the highest point on the knoll, most pronounced that a house on the summit would have a splendid view. Politely, they were shown the door.

Then came Annie Arkin and David Tilt, who walked every inch of the property before suggesting the knoll be preserved as a place to visit, have picnics, and even hold weddings. They also pointed out that a house placed just behind the knoll would be hidden from the valley below. These suggestions alone might have won over George and John, but Arkin Tilt Architects also had a reputation for environmentally enlightened design and the use of recycled materials.

No ornament, no fancy trim. Earthen walls and sensitive siting connect house and land in a way that makes the place memorable, reflecting a style that one of the project architects calls "farmhouse vernacular."

Wraparound wake-up call. The south-facing master bedroom overlooks an adjoining courtyard and lap pool. The tall bank of windows wrapping around the corner of the building provides unrestricted views of the hillside in the distance.

John's childhood memory of his grandmother's farmhouse in Maine was a seminal inspiration for this retreat, as were George's memories of a year in Tuscany. In putting substance to their ideas, the architects found John and George to be ideal clients. Rather than insisting on specific features in the house, they were more likely to ask their architects to meet broad design goals and performance standards. That gave the designers more freedom in responding creatively. Whenever John or George did have a specific idea, they would first try to understand what the architects had in mind before asking for a change. Nevertheless, they were not thoughtlessly compliant. George, for example, asked that the tower be moved from the rear of the house, where it had originally been drawn, to the front, where it had more presence. He also worked out the entire paving system and insisted on a Dutch-style front door. John involved himself extensively in the design of the beds, the window seats, and many of the counters.

Both the architects and the clients were rewarded for being open to ideas from others. Their builder, for example, sought out and remilled recycled lumber and learned how to pour concrete countertops to cut costs. Another architect who visited the site suggested a patio barbeque.

Old Materials, New Life

Old materials refashioned into contemporary uses bring with them an imprint of their former lives. To architects Annie Arkin and David Tilt, using salvaged materials proves that elegance and ecological sensitivity can be comfortable companions. This Dutch door, made from resawn Douglas fir timbers and hung with recycled hinges, is also a tribute to the thrifty sensibilities of vernacular farm buildings that both architects admire.

On the way to breakfast. Framed by this covered walkway, the western vista is John's favorite view. Straight ahead is an outdoor dining area protected by a trellis, while the ground-floor guest quarters are in the tower to the left.

Kitchen for all occasions. Simple finishes and efficient layout have long been the key features of a harvest kitchen. Farmers need a generalized space that's suitable for both formal celebrations and informal meals.

The Right Design

From the outset, Arkin envisioned several small buildings arranged around a central space, a theme she calls "farmhouse vernacular," which is borrowed from the way farm buildings typically develop over time. Arkin proposed three separate structures carefully placed around a series of connected courtyards and covered walkways, or "loggia." Although the three-story tower is the most visually dominant structure, the building that houses a great room and kitchen is actually larger. The third building, containing a study, master bedroom, and laundry, has the same proportions as the tower—one of them horizontal, the other vertical. Anchoring an open-sided courtyard is an elegant lap pool, made with an invisible edge that sends the eye out to the distant view.

The Ultimate Open Plan

Where the climate cooperates, there's no need for all rooms to be connected. Separating this residence into three structures creates courtyards, loggias, and porches. These outdoor rooms and covered walkways frame the views and fully integrate the landscape with the interior spaces. The kitchen and great room, oriented along cardinal points, enjoy beautiful natural light, while the bedrooms and pool are wrapped around the hill to set up the best views.

Great room

Covered walkway

Terrace

Kitchen

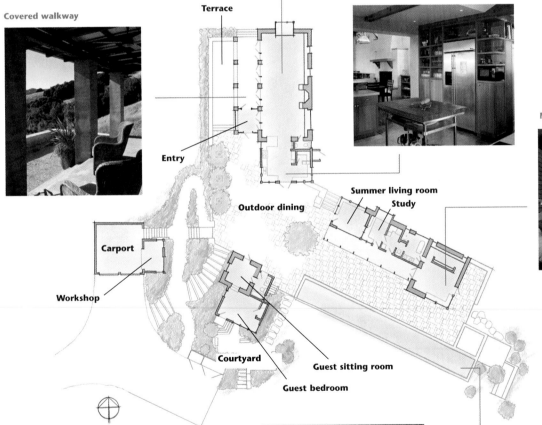

Entry

Master bedroom

Outdoor dining

Summer living room

Study

Carport

Workshop

Courtyard

Guest sitting room

Guest bedroom

Pool

Arkin's skillful arrangement of structures creates outdoor rooms that extend and enhance interior spaces. To get to the great room or kitchen, for instance, guests must cross an open courtyard between the tower and the main building. A loggia and terrace adjoining the great room encourage the use of outside as well as inside spaces, while the outdoor kitchen is particularly successful in creating flexible living space.

Reacting to their clients' profound affection for the land, the architects promoted the use of heavy earthen walls as a way to connect people architecturally to the site. They used a technique called "pise de terre" that involves mixing earth with a small amount of cement and spraying it through a nozzle to form walls—very much like the process used to make swimming pools and retaining walls with concrete. The material can be made largely from what's on the site, and it has great thermal qualities. Above all, it's permanent. The walls of Tip Top House have already survived one serious earthquake without a crack.

Interior partition walls of traditional board and batten offset the feel of heavy masonry and make it easier to route mechanical systems. With radiant-floor heat and the benefits of a huge thermal mass for both heating and cooling, there was no need for supply-and-return air ducts or radiators.

Multiplying the view. Without the visual obstruction of a conventional pool edge, the short view and long view become one. From some angles, the long view is actually doubled in the reflection of the pool.

Breaking bread takes center stage. The trellised eating area is conveniently served by both an indoor kitchen and an all-weather barbeque.

Memorable places are low maintenance. Durable materials that require little maintenance are central to a house capable of serving many generations. Walls were formed by shooting a mixture of earth and cement through a gun nozzle.

Sustainable style. Thick earthen walls and polished concrete floors make a significant thermal mass that absorbs the sun's heat, keeping rooms cool during the day and warm by night.

A door to the past. How can the passage of time and the touch of humanity be absorbed into a physical material? A new door built from old wood will always have an ineffable quality that new materials cannot match.

Wisconsin Corn Cribs

"During the design phase of this project, we traveled to Wisconsin for a family wedding," recalls architect Annie Arkin. "Driving into the countryside, we were struck by the beauty of the local corn cribs—slatted wood structures for corn storage that allow airflow—particularly with the setting sun filtering through them." This cribbing became an important material, serving as a perfect ventilating privacy screen at the carport and propane enclosure, and as an overlay on plywood and batten for light play and texture on a few key pieces at the terrace.

The Right Story

It's not usually possible to bootstrap history's patina, but Arkin's commitment to recycled materials successfully transplants the luster of age to a house that's barely a year old. The wood in the main ceilings came from old pickle barrels. The front door is redwood taken from old wine casks. Many of the bathroom and light fixtures were refurbished finds from an architectural salvage shop. Some of the counters are recycled bowling alleys.

Even better than importing history is making it. George and John host guests every other weekend—including a number of children—and they urge friends to use the house even when they're away. Typically guests arrive to candles and flowers in the suite in the base of the tower, a private location allowing late arrivals and dawn departures. As the number of guests increases, a study, a sitting room, and even a bookshelf can be converted into guest accommodations. The house can host large groups comfortably but still feel intimate when numbers are small.

As visually restorative as the terrain may be, John's greatest enjoyment comes from actually working the land. In addition to a bounty of homegrown flowers, he preserves olives that he raises on the property. His gifts of this harvest help lessen the reluctance that guests invariably feel in leaving and encourage them to make a speedy return.

Inspired inventions. Fold-down footholds give access to a captain's bed designed to fit within the thickness of the walls. A built-in doghouse has access from inside and out.

Hanging out in between. There is always indoors and out, but with thick-walled buildings there may be an in-between choice. From within the protective haven of these walls, this window bed gives access to the full drama of the terrain in all weather conditions.

Rural Rehab

Like many New Yorkers, Jean and Ed Stoler sustained their dream for a country existence with weekend outings to their upstate camp, a poorly proportioned saltbox in a style Jean called "motel modern." In time, they began making plans to leave Manhattan and make a permanent move to the country. The question was where. Although they had the camp, it had neither charm nor enough space for visiting children and grandchildren. No, the Stolers would need something else entirely.

Just bring me the paper. After 12 years of spending weekends here, the owners were very familiar with the beauty of the pond on the property. But what they didn't expect was how much they would enjoy the new screened porch that overlooks it. In season, it's a place to eat and relax.

Scenic symmetry. Repeated patterns and symmetrical shapes disguise any hint of the original camp's lack of grace. The proportions of the final design give a cottagelike feel to this substantial house.

Model home.
Although the Stolers at first couldn't imagine renovating their tired country house, architect Dennis Wedlick's model of what a redesigned house might look like helped them see untapped possibilities.

Their search for another house proved longer and more difficult than they might have guessed. In the end, the Stolers were surprised to discover that the ungainly camp might actually be the start of a perfect country home. All it took was a timely dinner with the right guest and a few well-chosen words of advice.

You Mean This Old Place?

Anticipating a protracted search for a new house, Jean had given up her 25-year career in fashion design, moved to the camp, and set up a mosaic-tile shop in the village nearby. With tiling and teaching paying the bills, Jean spent her extra time scouting out real estate possibilities. Ed, still living in New York, commuted on weekends.

What the Stolers imagined for their dream spot could be summed up in four words: privacy with a pond. Unfortunately, houses they saw that met those criteria needed modifications before the Stolers could move in. And invariably, the cost of those modifications made the deal unworkable. After a year of fruitless looking, two events precipitated a promising call to action: Ed lost his job, and architect Dennis Wedlick was invited to dinner.

A good friend of Jean's sister, Dennis had long been an acquaintance of the Stolers. Over dinner, they told him their story. The company where Ed worked was being sold, encouraging them to think about a permanent relocation sooner than they had expected. And yet nothing on the market seemed to fit their needs. A familiar conundrum, thought Dennis, and he urged them to look no further. "You will never find a place as nice as the one you already have," he told them. "Renovate." Jean and Ed realized that they would have to renovate one way or another, and they tried to imagine how they could possibly transform the characterless camp into their country dream home.

Design on a Dime

After interviewing several architects, Jean and Ed discovered that Dennis alone seemed to really understand what they wanted to do. Determined to work with him, Jean asked what they could do to save money. He suggested they each make separate wish lists, good advice for any homeowner considering a house project. Clarity always saves money.

Beyond the two basics of pond and privacy, Jean wanted three things: an open feel within the house, a heated garage with studio, and an entirely different look on the outside.

Homeowner's Journal

❝ I was close to burnout on fashion design when I visited a tourist attraction in France called Pique Assiette or 'broken pieces,'" says Jean Stoler. "It was a little house right next to Chartres Cathedral that had been completely tiled by the owner. The floors, walls, ceilings, and even the furniture were covered with beautiful mosaics made from tiny pieces of broken crockery. It was exquisite, and I realized instantly that I wanted to learn how to do this. ❞

Upstairs, downstairs.
Views of the main living
area from a second-floor
walkway help to weave
upper and lower spaces
into a coherent whole.
The baronial stone fire-
place was on Ed Stoler's
short list of wants in a
renovated house.

FAUX LATTICE

Looking for something a little different to replace the tired vertical-board siding on the Stolers' camp, architect Dennis Wedlick settled on a substrate of fiber-cement panels overlaid with a lattice of narrow painted boards. Too expensive to be used on the whole house, this layered treatment is used to emphasize new and enlarged parts of the façade with an unusual character and texture.

For his part, Ed wanted a real stone fireplace, his own sanctuary where he could relax and watch television, and a screened porch where they could enjoy views of the pond without being devoured by bugs. Dennis and Jean quickly concluded that Dennis would focus on the structure while Jean would work on the interior. Dennis was open to everything Jean brought to the design process, acting as an architectural safety net as well as a reliable sounding board.

Exterior Excellence

With a few Zen-like strokes, Dennis transformed the threadbare camp into a beautiful home. The badly pitched saltbox roof was mirrored to become a nicely proportioned gable. This might have looked awkward had the garage addition not been roofed to match. Without being slavishly symmetrical, the addition creates a balanced house appropriately scaled to the pond it adjoins. Two distinctive sets of stadiumlike stairs give access to a deck that runs the entire length of the house, providing plenty of places to sit and enjoy the cattails.

Casual formality. Architect Dennis Wedlick and owner Jean Stoler created a relaxed design to announce the formal entry to this country cottage. Using half of the wraparound stairs for flower display softens their contemporary sizzle.

In spite of the many entry options, the formal front door is clearly marked by a distinctive round window, the only curve in the entire design. Once over the threshold, you have a view straight through the house to a back door and another porch, this one with a wisteria-covered pergola.

One of the surprises for Jean and Ed is the way Dennis's design connects them with all sides of their house. They seldom visited the backyard before the renovation, but Jean now has a large herb garden and sitting area there directly off the kitchen. Indeed, she now spends a good deal of time collaborating with a landscaper on planting beds around the yards.

Country Comfort

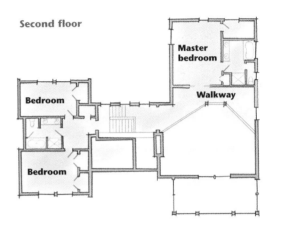

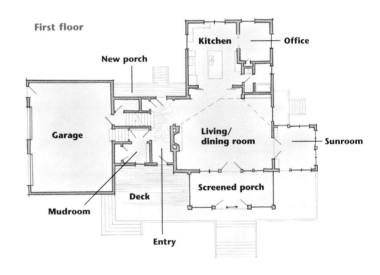

Absentee Goldbrick. Like so many people enthralled with landscaping design, Jean is rarely found in the idyllic scenarios she is so busy creating. A creative green thumb never rests.

Intimate Interior

With Dennis backing her up, Jean was ready to follow her creative impulses. A huge set of barn doors allows the kitchen to be open to the main living area and take advantage of its pond view but to be closed when the kitchen is a mess or when the cook doesn't want to be disturbed. Not that Jean is ashamed of the kitchen—she designed it. The cabinets are custom built to her sketches. She specified the cherry and soapstone counters and not only designed but also built the little sitting area overlooking the herb garden.

Timeless ingenuity. Sliding barn doors are actually moveable walls too big to put on hinges. By detailing them as barn doors, these beauties bring an agrarian feel to this contemporary design. They also allow the cook privacy when appropriate.

Staying connected. The Stolers located their master bedroom suite over the garage, but easy access to the rest of the house prevents them from feeling isolated. A French door from the bedroom opens to stairs leading down to the entry and main living space and up to a second-floor walkway.

If the project brought with it a satisfying collaboration between architect and client, Dennis also played advocate for his own ideas on a few occasions. When the soaring cathedral ceiling came into the budget-cutting crosshairs, Dennis took a stand. He was gentler but still clear in his insistence on the proportions of the entry hall and doorways. He helped Jean find a place on the stairs for the bookshelves she wanted to crowd in next to the fireplace. In all cases, Jean now concedes she's glad she listened.

Taking a tub. Inspired by design magazines, Jean Stoler had for years dreamed of having a whirlpool bath beneath a skylight. Architect Dennis Wedlick made it happen, and it's now one of her favorite spots in the house.

Know Thyself

The secret to Ed and Jean's happiness is in their mutual discovery and acceptance of who they are. This was particularly evident during the remaking of their home. For instance, Ed is a scholarly neat-nick, while Jean is a messy artist. In designing this house, Ed provided Jean with a studio (where he never goes), and Jean provided Ed with his study/refuge (where she never goes).

Accepting their differences helped to bond them, and they had plenty of practice during construction. Ed and Jean decided to save money by living on site. This turned out to mean one room, accessible by ladder, shared with a dog, a hot plate, most of the dust, and all of the noise. Jean says that keeping a close watch on the project during the day prevented a lot of errors. By night, they abused the hospitality of friends.

Today the Stolers are a couple of happy, redirected ex-urbanites. Ed is almost finished getting his teaching certificate, and Jean, in spite of a thriving tile business, is contemplating a new career in residential design. Would they do it again? "Never!" says Ed. Then, more candidly: "Unless Jean really wanted to. I suppose then, after kicking and screaming, I'd probably go along. I've come to appreciate that every day is a new day when married to Jean."

Country house chutzpa. There's something about a casual style that gives homeowners the confidence to jump right in. After watching others construct the kitchen she designed, Jean couldn't resist direct involvement and built this sitting area herself.

Studios, Offices, and Workshops

PLACES TO WORK—whether for a vocation, avocation, or just paying the bills—have become increasingly important considerations in today's households. During design, many homeowners are as articulate about what they want in their studios, studies, and workshops as they are about their kitchens.

For the right personality and the right occupation, a home office or studio can work well. It helps if the workspace is well differentiated from the rest of the house and can be easily closed off. Otherwise, the at-home worker will effectively be on the job round the clock, feeling guilty about undone chores and subject to calls from clients and colleagues at all hours. Those who work at home often place the office at a distance from the center of the house. This gives them the sensation of "going to work" at the start of the day and "closing the office" in the evening. On the other hand, a home studio or shop allows those in a creative line of work to act on that "Eureka!" moment whenever it arrives, regardless of time or day.

After 25 years without a workspace, a New York City fashion designer who moved to a house in the country discovered a whole new dimension to her creativity when she had enough room for her own private studio.

A successful home studio creates an environment suited to the task at hand. An artisan welder may not need a great view, but generous windows and an inspiring landscape may be just the ticket for a landscape artist.

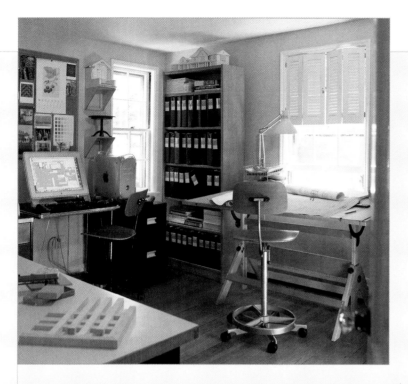

A workspace on the second floor of this tower is ideally located—near the main house but still separate. Being able to close the door and walk away at the end of the day is an important feature in a home office or studio.

Computers and access to the Internet allow small design studios, traditionally needing large drafting and library spaces, to be happily housed in a standard-sized bedroom.

In addition to a good work surface, ample shelving, and good lighting, the most important feature for the workspace is a window with a refreshing view. Stretching the eyes and getting "outside" of the work has been shown to increase creativity and productivity. Almost as much as a good coffee maker.

Those who are passionate about their interests respond to spaces that are equally inspired. This flower studio encourages its talented and motivated owner to work at the highest possible level.

People who are serious about cooking will customize their kitchens to accommodate their personal culinary pursuits. This baking station includes a lowered stone counter to make it easier to knead and roll dough.

Going Native

Bill and Georgia Hoffmann had never thought much about adobe before happening into Taos on their "where shall we retire someday" tour. Suddenly they were wondering if a big-building architect from San Francisco might trade in his successful commercial career for a one-man design practice in New Mexico. They bought the land for a dream that was still 10 years off. Then, six months later, they decided not to wait.

Gallery entrance. A raised entry with a hand-carved door houses a variety of art objects that give guests a taste of what lies ahead. Adobe walls needn't be structural to be thick.

Come in out of the sun. Generous landscaping on the street side of the house suggests a welcome oasis in the Southwestern heat.

With no prospective clients locally, it made sense for Bill's first project to be his own house. True to the stereotype of a spendthrift architect, his initial design was over budget. Unlike most architects, however, his response to this situation was very much in keeping with vernacular tradition—roll up your sleeves and join the fray. Bill and Georgia had already studied adobe design and history. Now they schooled themselves in the actual construction, which unlocked a whole new venue for personalizing their home.

Taos is filled with failed attempts to personalize the historic adobe style without corrupting it. Like any vernacular style, it's the philosophy as much as the construction techniques that makes the difference. Maybe it was their hands-on approach or maybe Bill and Georgia were Pueblo Indians in a former life, but their first effort has a wonderfully authentic feel.

Walls Like Melting Butter

Few building traditions connect a house to the site like adobe. Mined directly from the ground, the earth and water mixture is cast into blocks, baked by the sun, and then piled into walls and covered with a thick layer of stucco. The process allows a great deal of flexibility and creativity, and as

LESSONS FROM THE PAST

Adobe was a leader in sustainable and energy-conscious architecture long before those terms were part of every architect's vocabulary. Made on the building site from natural and renewable materials, adobe is easily formed into massive walls that offer excellent thermal efficiency. Yet adobe is far from being the only traditional building style that still has something to offer. With a few adjustments, vernacular styles as diverse as New England's saltbox and Florida's cracker houses can be updated to perform well in today's environmentally conscious world.

House as sculpture. The handmade shapes of traditional adobe recall the sensual, undulating forms of a Henry Moore sculpture.

his crews were shaping the walls in the heat, Bill would periodically shout out, "Make 'em look like melting buttah!" Doors and windows seemed to sink into the massive walls even as the roof beams and rain scuppers protrude from above. In the Southwestern light, these are the features that produce the dramatic shadows for which adobe is prized.

Using an X-shaped layout aligned with the sun, Bill was able to create a cool outdoor space for every time of day. Even though it needed to be inviting, he let the street façade face south since he knew people wouldn't be lingering there. The cooler sides of the house are given over to a private patio and garden. The separate garage, cleverly designed with an attached shop to obscure the garage door, creates a welcoming entry court.

Chasing shadows. Careful orientation of the house on the site and thoughtful room layout create cool patios and gardens that give refuge from the sun at all times of the day.

Designed for a crowd. From the raised entry, an open layout beyond invites guests to socialize. Several generous doorways provide easy traffic flow to the patios.

UP REALLY CLOSE

A Better Entertainment Center

Repurposing old-fashioned features is a way to preserve form and function in a vernacular design. Good examples include widow's walks, root cellars, backstairs, and, in Southwestern adobes, *alacenas*. Traditionally, *alacenas* were wooden cupboards built into the thick adobe walls. In contemporary renovations, they have been adapted to hold televisions, books, computers…and sometimes even firewood.

The front door opens onto a raised foyer that gives people arriving an immediate sense of the graceful relationship between the house and its sloping site. By generous placement of glazed doors and ample windows, the space seems to flow continuously from the cool interior out into the shaded gardens. This effect is furthered by Bill's use of sandstone pavers both inside and out. Indeed, until he saw the first invoice, he had specified sandstone sills at all the doors so the floor treatment could flow uninterrupted right through to the patio.

Instinctively, Bill understood that the thick-walled building method begged for sculptural treatment. Into the chunkier walls he designed window seats, art niches, and *alacenas*, the Spanish word for storage built into the wall. *Alacenas* are used in the bathrooms and bedrooms to eliminate medicine cabinets and television furniture. On the television *alacena* in the master bedroom, two spirit dolls made after a vacation to Africa are fashioned into cabinet door pulls.

When the Money Runs Out

Part of the appeal of a historic house is that it reflects the conditions of the era in which it was built. So, in hindsight, a tight budget may have been the best thing for the Hoffmanns' adobe design. After all, mortgages weren't available when the Pueblo Indians built traditional adobes. The trick to getting what you want, then as now, is being creative with limited resources. Bill and Georgia couldn't wait to get involved.

For starters, they hired Mark Wilson, a contractor with a lot of adobe experience who was willing to let his clients help with the construction. Georgia quickly established herself as the resident color czar when she asked Raymond, the plasterer, to add a capful of sienna to his plaster. Dubious at first, he soon realized that this subtle tinting was making his work look older and richer than most new adobes. After that, no one was surprised to see Georgia staining the roof beams, called *vigas,* with a homemade finish that muted the fluorescent color of the Douglas fir, or, later in the process, painting Southwestern patterns about the house and creating colorful pillows for the window seats.

Adaptation aesthetics. Fireplaces were built into corners in traditional adobes. When subsequent renovations called for the elimination of an adjacent wall, enough was saved to preserve both fireplace and corner. The resulting wing-walls were so appealing that today they are incorporated into designs at the outset.

Fearlessly homemade. The homeowners adapted African folk figures for cabinet pulls, made shades from rolled fabric, and fashioned affordable ornaments with techniques gleaned from local crafts shows.

A touch of dirt. Modern plaster is too bright to be authentic. Using just a capful of sienna in the mix mutes the harsh whiteness and produces warm tones of age.

Folk art in the kitchen. To create the feeling of a country kitchen, Bill designed cabinetry to look like furniture, adding fish pulls on drawers and round corner shelves to display crockery. The fish theme is continued with homemade sconces over the patio door.

Homeowner's Journal

❝ Bill and I are fearlessly creative, and since we rarely like store bought, it's a good thing we have the ability to adapt. If we can't afford it, then we'll build it ourselves. When we were pressed for time, we decided to turn existing art objects into fixtures, adding tin, wood, whatever it took to make the light work. ❞

Hands On

For his part, Bill decided to tackle the kitchen cabinets. Learning cabinetmaking as he went, his dedication to craft yielded a kitchen that looks neither crudely homemade nor slickly store bought, a perfect complement to the adobe walls and hand-hewn beams. To avoid the trendy magazine look that dates most contemporary kitchens, he detailed the counters to look like freestanding furniture. For instance, the peninsula counter separating the dining area from the kitchen has been designed to look like a sideboard. Upper cabinets are kept to a minimum.

Storage and the refrigerator are tucked away in an oversized pantry, allowing both to be convenient without compromising the rural atmosphere of the kitchen. Georgia's paint treatment completes the refrigerator's transformation—no need for a high-priced designer model here.

With only a week before the bank inspection, Georgia went into creative overdrive. Discarding the catalogues, she quickly discovered a dozen affordable ways to enhance a bare light bulb. Inexpensive clay fish, quickly painted masks, and locally made trinkets were transformed into imaginative light shades. A thrift store yielded an old Italian chandelier, which, after a little rewiring, became the perfect counterpoint to their rustic dining area.

This hands-on approach engaged the Hoffmanns' creativity well beyond the need to save money. Time spent in the local craft shops inspired Georgia to experiment, and she was soon producing folded-metal mirrors, freestanding light fixtures, and

Refurbished lighting in a relaxed layout. Discovered in
a thrift store, this Italianate chandelier saved the owner
money and provided a fun afternoon of antiquing. The
traditional broken walls define the dining room without
interrupting the flow of space.

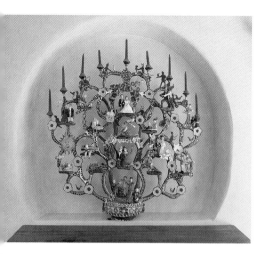

Better than photos on the fridge.
Bill and Georgia make a Tree of Life each Christmas to reflect meaningful family events of the year just passed. With its record of births, deaths, and marriages for one year so remarkable, the tree was ensconced permanently in its own wall niche.

Aligned with the Sun

Main floor

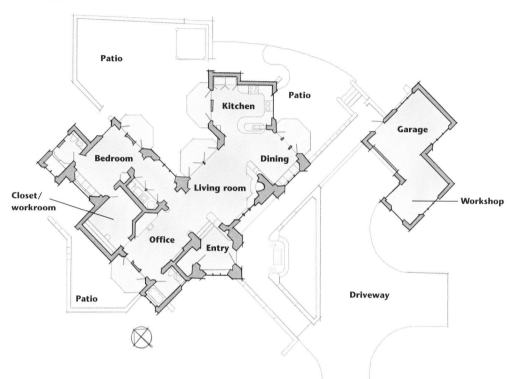

Patio

Kitchen

Patio

Garage

Bedroom

Dining

Closet/
workroom

Living room

Workshop

Office

Entry

Patio

Driveway

bold new color schemes. Meanwhile, Bill took a carving course to expand his abilities in traditional woodworking.

Integrating a modern lifestyle with a historic building method is a worthwhile challenge. Vernacular architecture is defined as "of the place, of the culture, and *by the people.*" Crucial to the success of this project was the Hoffmanns' ability to simultaneously be on-site students as well as supervisors and homeowners. From its orientation to the sun rather than to an arbitrary street grid all the way to its carefully detailed parts filled with local art, this is an adobe that successfully connects the present to the past.

Going to sleep was impossible.
What was originally a guest bedroom, Bill's studio is awash in the flow of space and light so typical of his designs. Guests now enjoy a separate *casita,* or "little house."

Upgrading ancient wisdom.
Bill attended a woodcarving
class before making this gate
and studied museum originals
to make the ladder. The scuppers, however, are a product of
modern engineering.

Mediterranean influence in Santa Fe. When they travel,
the Hoffmanns look carefully for indigenous design solutions. In Greece, they found a retractable awning like this
one that can be operated by one person.

Magical Makeover

If ever there was an inspired house fairy tale, it would be the story of Allison and Warner McConaughey's magical makeover of this derelict American foursquare. While still a young designer and builder, Warner purchased the Atlanta, Georgia, property for $17,000 at a tax auction and proceeded to renovate it with little more than credit cards and a lot of hard work. Ten years later, a foursquare princess overlooks a pleasant, tree-lined street where once only "toads" lurked.

Accidental genius. The original builders probably gave little thought to locating the houses on their sites, but the effect is striking. Perfectly aligned porches spanning the entire block created a comfortable zone where people can socialize, promoting neighborly feelings.

Toad or princess? Not every old house is worth retrieving, but there are certainly many unclaimed bargains in derelict houses. The owner bought this one at a tax auction and restored it on a low budget.

House for a Neighborhood

The American foursquare is an offshoot of Prairie-style architecture that flourished in the first part of the 20th century and spread to both coasts by way of pattern books authored in the Midwest. Typically, the simple hip-roofed box contained four rooms on each of two floors. In the early 1900s, this style was a good match for Atlanta. Facing the street, the straightforward plan opened onto a shaded sweep of porch that spanned the entire front of the house. Affordable and comfortable, foursquares quickly lined the streets of many not-so-wealthy neighborhoods. Small lots and uniform setbacks made these houses look something like big kids huddled on a small bench. But when homeowners sought the shade of their porches, they soon realized that the alignment also created perfect conditions for neighborly interaction.

Big box with all the trimmings. The American foursquare is an unassuming style, without dramatic façades or cantilevers. Its lasting appeal stems from ample, light-filled rooms with delightful detailing both inside and out. With mature trees and an elevated front lawn, this one is a rare find.

If not original, compatible. The rear of the house was too far gone to restore. This new porch design is sympathetically proportioned and detailed, and it shades and de-emphasizes the modern windows and doors.

Foursquare Classic

Second floor

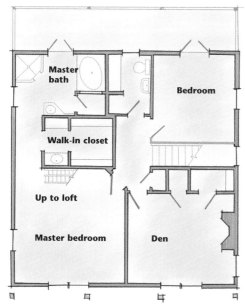

Master bath

Bedroom

Walk-in closet

Up to loft

Master bedroom

Den

First floor

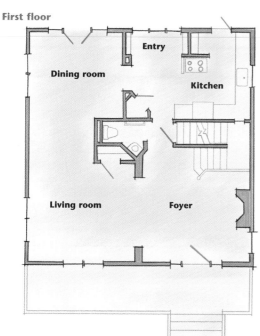

Entry

Dining room

Kitchen

Living room

Foyer

By the time Warner won his toad at auction, the porch and any neighborly feeling were long gone. Undaunted, he set out to revive the latter by restoring the former. Older houses and existing neighborhoods are good bets when looking for that elusive sense of place. In spite of the property's terrible condition, 80 years of just being there was still a priceless feature. Warner realized that ignoring this history would be throwing away the most important part of his purchase.

He developed a design strategy that would restore the historic exterior on the front and sides of the house while reconfiguring the back and the interior to suit a more contemporary lifestyle. His strategy included lots of determination, skill, and time, but very little cash. Every move had to count. In the single act of rebuilding the front porch, Warner re-established critical relationships between the interior life of the house, the front yard, the street, and his neighbors. By re-creating the dignity and simple grace of the exterior, he set a tone that has influenced the entire street. Today, most of the formerly run-down houses in this neighborhood have been refurbished.

Warm welcome. An entry hall with stairs and a fireplace is an ageless indication of warmth and hospitality, even in Georgia, where a fire is seldom required. Chairs around the hearth encourage guests to sit and stay awhile.

Details Make the Difference

Because the front—especially the porch—was carefully detailed to look original, one presumes the whole house has been restored with equal fidelity. As you enter the foyer, this impression is reinforced with small but clever design moves. Where walls have been modified or removed, the floor has been patched with identical flooring taken from elsewhere in the house. The baseboard, picture molding, and other trim are seamlessly connected and integrated with new walls. A new opening into the living room is bracketed with the same Doric columns found on the porch. Taken together, these details create the feeling of a coherent 1900s interior, even though it was built a century later. Out in back, a new, two-story porch designed and built by the young couple could easily have been part of the original house.

Historic handling of contemporary spaces. With one wall removed and an opening in the other enlarged, this view from the dining room extends all the way to the front door. Open, flowing space need not corrupt the traditional character if the furnishings are properly chosen and arranged.

Seamless transformation. Missing windows on the street side were replaced with units salvaged from the rear. The broad new opening to the living room is detailed to match existing trim in the house, and the Doric column is identical to the ones holding up the porch.

Small Beginnings

Warner McConaughey came across this kitchen range before he'd even seen the Atlanta foursquare he would eventually renovate. The range didn't work, but Warner knew it could be repaired. It was a deal, and he tucked it away for the future. It was this ability to see the intrinsic value in an abandoned object that later guided him to the tax-auction purchase of his house. In it, he saw enough of the original building fabric to make the house worthy of attention. Like his kitchen range, all it needed to become fully operational (even contemporary) once again was a sensitive fix.

The same effect is harder to achieve in a kitchen because modern equipment conflicts with traditional fixtures and fittings. Warner's solution was to place a stunning period range in a central location and then design the kitchen around it. The range is the first and most dominant thing you see as you enter the room, and it sets the mood for the whole kitchen. Adding to the effect, Italian tile, matte granite counters, traditional cabinetry, and an old-fashioned sink neutralize the modern recessed lights and stainless-steel appliances.

Upstairs, there are additional examples of how minor design moves achieve major effects. In the master bedroom, for example, a bit of unused attic space has been cleverly converted into a study loft. The loft concept is decidedly modern, but here it's successfully integrated with the help of a wrought-iron banister that matches the bed's headboard. Another modern room, the walk-in closet, almost feels original due to the careful use of tile, trim, and a built-in bureau. Incorporating period furniture as built-ins is an excellent way to meet logistical needs while enhancing the feel and sense of place.

In the privacy of the bedroom. Only here did Warner feel he could create something as modern as a loft. An iron railing that matches the headboard on the bed helps integrate this modern feature with a century-old foursquare design.

Updated bed design. Although historically the canopy bed was designed to keep warmth in and everything else out, today's modern HVAC systems make them obsolete. Loath to give up this "room within a room," designers of every stripe have modernized the canopy. This steel cube is perfectly proportioned for the higher ceilings in this house.

A walk-in worth waiting for. Built-in bureaus with tile surround give this closet more of a dressing room feel. Tile at floor level means the usual scuffing associated with shoe storage is no longer a problem.

Old Glories

Using building parts from bygone times can create effects that would cost too much to produce today, presuming you could find the skilled labor that still remembers how. This sink surround and toothbrush and soap holders all came from architectural salvage outlets. Only the tile and faucet are new. As the prices of salvaged building materials go up, the profitability of making reproductions brings more choice to the marketplace.

The McConaugheys used a lot of tile throughout the house. By incorporating high-end ceramics sparingly in a composition of mostly ordinary tile, they have achieved an elegant effect at moderate cost. Little touches, such as a period toothbrush holder and soap dish from a local salvage shop, enhance this feeling of an old, well-lived-in residence. As always, successful design comes from an integrated vision, not a checklist of ingredients.

Up to date. Vintage fixtures, brick-tile walls, and mosaics on the floor give historic ambiance to the extra bathroom. But because this master bathroom is used daily, it calls for contemporary materials used in a new but sympathetic design. The door (at left) leads to a porch overlooking the garden.

Cinderella Color Choice

It was about the time the kitchen was nearing completion that Warner met Allison, an interior designer, on a first date. After dinner and a show, Warner brought Allison home to help choose a color for his new bachelor kitchen. Today, it's their kitchen. Although conventional wisdom holds that renovation projects stress matrimonial bonds, this one actually precipitated their union. When the client, architect, builder, interior designer, plumber, and trim carpenter are all living under the same roof, the odds of creating a memorable place increase dramatically. Of course, that only happens in a fairy tale.

The magic in this house goes beyond the McConaugheys' ability to integrate old and new affordably. Their real gift is an ability to see and feel a bygone place, know that they could live there, and bring it back so that it reflects their own lives and personalities. Magic or not, the results of their work will live happily ever after.

Living in the city. What better indication that this house has been fully revitalized than this beautiful yard and garden. Lush outdoor spaces are what make dense urban living possible.

Eclectic elegance. Allison believes that interior décor should reflect the personalities of the homeowners even as it works gracefully with the architectural style. These timeless tea boxes staged on the upstairs den mantel do just that.

Thicker Than Water

As wholehearted sports enthusiasts, Connie and Bill Carlson appreciate the power of team-work. Their winning strategy in the homebuilding game is something anyone can take to heart: First, know what you want, then decide who can help you get there.

Just settling into a recently renovated house, Connie and Bill weren't shopping for either property or another house when Bill spotted this lot. Yet even before he stopped the car, Bill knew he wanted the view at the end of the winding drive.

Unfair competition. Even the latest and largest plasma television has a tough time upstaging this view of Alki Beach. Fortunately for the networks, there are plenty of overcast nights in Seattle.

With an old friend working in real estate, he took two days away from his dental practice to research every comparable piece of real estate in West Seattle. Convinced that this was an overlooked jewel, his attention shifted to who could help him make it happen.

All in the Family

There are two kinds of family when it comes to making houses: blood relatives and professionals who act like kin. The Carlsons are blessed with both. Bill's father had been a contractor. His brother, Dave, is a cabinetmaker. Connie's sister, Layne, is a kitchen and bath designer married to Jed Johnson, a general contractor. With that kind of family involvement in the trades, an inspired collaboration was right around the corner.

Although Layne and Jed had worked with many architects, it was their opinion that Lane Williams was the only designer for this job (and not just because he had the same first name). Nevertheless, given the narrow site, steep grades, and badly designed house already on the lot, Bill and Connie

Picture perfect, patio perfect. Bill saw the potential for a perfect patio the instant he set foot on the property. Part of experiencing any view is the environment from which we enjoy it, and this patio excels on both counts.

ARCHITECT'S CORNER

ROOF LOADING

"When filled with water, the spa and pool weigh about 25,000 lb.—comparable to parking five large cars on the roof," says project architect Lane Williams. "Though I have faith in my engineer, I did ask the owner to remove his Porsche from the garage the day they filled the pool."

interviewed several others before hiring Williams. Besides being the family favorite, he was the most articulate about how the project could meet site restrictions, seismic requirements, and budget limitations.

With Williams as the architect, Jed acting as general contractor, and Layne designing the kitchen and baths, Connie and Bill were comfortably situated in the lap of an extended design/build family.

House to Match a Lifestyle

Connie and Bill, both active athletes, train daily for their chosen sports. A generous-sized exercise room occupies most of the ground floor. When not at speed with their work-hard-play-hard approach to life, they are relaxing or informally entertaining on their patio. "PT," or patio time, held top billing on their architectural wish list.

With a natural enthusiasm for plants and landscaping, Bill focused his attention on the patio environment. He set very high goals for landscaping and even brought plantings from their previous home. Other than patio perfection, Bill

Who needs a column? Hanging from steel supports, this curved canopy softens the leading corner of the house and marks a separate entry to Connie's studio.

Japanese mask on a Mediterranean face. The homeowners liked Spanish Colonial; the architect had a passion for Japanese. The strength of the design comes from wedding aspects of both.

just wanted to be able to see the view as soon as he entered the front door and, to some extent, from every room of the house. Connie, like most homeowners keen on design, had gathered a collection of favorite pages from *Architectural Digest*. They detailed her preference for Spanish, Mexican, and Mediterranean design. Specifically, she wanted stucco walls, a tiled roof, glass block, and, in a less stylistic vein, a lap pool. She also needed space for her home occupation as a beautician and stylist, as well as a studio for her artwork.

A Winning Team

With virtually no wiggle room, the thin lot starts out as little more than a cut in the curb. A narrow drive leads to parking for two cars in front of a garage and house that together consume the full buildable width of the site. Once the existing building was removed, Williams was able to create an open floor plan that met all of Connie and Bill's needs.

Crowded Shorelines Require Focused Views

This narrow lot with close neighbors on either side benefits from attention to window placement and view lines. The living spaces and patio are pushed to the view end of the lot, while the office, entry, and utility spaces are arranged in the site's center. Creative landscaping provides lush nearby vistas even as the bamboo and other plantings ensure privacy. The experience of the overall house includes short, middle, and distant views.

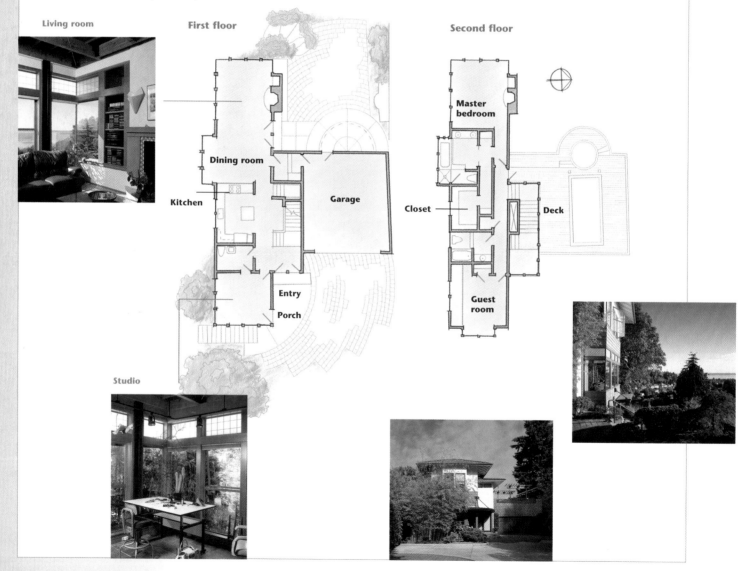

Living room

First floor

Second floor

Dining room

Kitchen

Garage

Master bedroom

Closet

Deck

Guest room

Entry

Porch

Studio

The view overlooking Alki Beach awaits as you open the front door but only because Layne's kitchen design incorporates upper cabinets higher than the standard 18 in. over the countertop. The kitchen is an elegant galley design consistent with Bill and Connie's casual cooking habits. Layne concentrated her efforts more in the bathrooms where high-style tiling and glass enclosures recall the southwestern look Connie requested. The main room, with its latticework of exposed joists above, offers sweeping views of the water and the mountains beyond.

While no one would call this house Mediterranean, Williams's use of stucco, plaster, and wood dovetailed perfectly with Connie's folder of magazine pages. When it came to color and finishes, Williams urged Connie to be bold. And bold she was: green ceilings and multichromatic slate that picks up colors throughout the house.

Sucked in by the scenery. Even from 45 ft. away, a striking view is visible as soon as you open the etched-glass front door. Upper cabinets mounted well above the countertop help keep sight lines open.

Constantly changing wallpaper. Every room in the house has access to the western vista. This creates a coherent sense of place while providing great sunset views for the homeowners.

Cleans up well. A seamless glass shower enclosure allows uninterrupted appreciation of the tile design as it marches around the bathroom. The architect insisted that colors be bold.

Logo for light lovers.
Connie freely admits that her business logo was inspired by a pagan symbol for the sun. As an inspiration for patio lights, it continues to symbolize the importance of the sun in the lives of these homeowners.

Every entry a memory. Brought in from Arizona, these knotty-pine doors recall the Mexican aesthetics Bill and Connie are so fond of.

Detailing Where It Counts

This beautifully veneered desk in bird's-eye maple goes well beyond what the architect had specified. Built by David Carlson, the homeowner's brother, the desk got more attention than other built-ins—and with good reason. This level of detailing and craftsmanship, along with a very careful selection of materials, is immediately apparent to whoever sits down to use it. That kind of intimacy is not the case with a stereo cabinet or even a personalized bureau (which, in this house, were also crafted by brother David). When Bill Carlson draws up a chair and starts to work, in a way he is also making contact with his brother.

The lap pool, located at the base of a three-story wall in the original design, was eventually moved to the roof of the garage. Connie was dubious about the choice of pool, a resistance-type installation that uses moving water to simulate an infinitely long pool. But cost concerns and a successful test swim brought her around. The final design meets building codes and saves money, and the adjacent hot tub provides sweeping views between workouts.

Collaboration between architect and homeowner reached a high point in the way the house and landscaping work together to make the most of the view while still preserving privacy. Williams's building configuration provides three great places to enjoy the panoramic vistas: the western rooms, the patio, and the garage-top "tubscape." But these and other architectural triumphs are substantially enhanced by Bill's landscaping. In addition to the plantings, Bill designed a fountain that helps to create a feeling of seclusion on the patio. And the near-magical transition from roaring traffic on the road to the tranquility in the entry court is largely the result of Bill's plantings.

Better Than a Contract

The clear communication and efficient construction that characterized this project were the result of something beyond the usual contracts and design documents. It was the people. Everyone on the team had worked with or already knew the others. Equally important, the homeowners and the architect expressed their design objectives clearly so everyone could get behind them.

Before the project was even off the drafting table, contractor Jed Johnson was working on construction details. As with any clan, family members knew they could never really hide from their work. So, when an earthquake measuring 6.1 on the Richter scale struck the area, what might have resulted in internecine warfare merely presented an opportunity for Connie to tease Jed. On the phone she implied disaster before confessing that the building—including the elevated pool and tub—had sailed through with hardly a creak.

Never forget the short view. With neighbors packed in like birds on a wire, care must be given to the short view as well as the panorama. Attention to landscaping creates a feeling of seclusion even in the middle of the crowd.

Growing to the music of water. The sounds made by this beautiful fountain seem to have entranced the adjacent landscaping. More important, it screens the sounds of neighbors on their nearby deck.

Impulse Buy

After living in four previous homes, John and Mollie Byrnes had no intention of creating another. They had settled comfortably into a condominium where they assumed they would stay for good. But then one Sunday, after a visit with family and friends in nearby Rockport, Massachusetts, they decided to take a scenic route home. Unexpectedly, they happened on an overgrown lot in a small subdivision within smelling distance of the ocean. Fighting through the brambles with growing excitement, they soon found themselves climbing a rock outcropping so their cell phone signal could reach the real estate agent.

Striking details in a simple room. Like two eyes above the cherry mantel and media center, the two interior windows allow sunlight from a dramatic skylight to penetrate an upstairs office.

They may have kidded each other about not leaving their condo unless it was in a pine box, but John and Mollie were about to plunge into a new house project again. They were lucky enough to team up with architect Paul MacNeely of the Boston firm Jeremiah Eck Architects.

Inspiration Comes with the Job

Paul draws his design inspiration from both the site and the clients. After an initial meeting with the Byrnes, he went to Rockport and spent hours exploring the property. Although the site doesn't have a direct view of the water, the sounds and smell of the ocean cast a magical tranquility over this rocky, tree-covered hillock. MacNeely focused immediately on creating a choreography of house and driveway. He protected the house from a direct view from the street, leaving only the roof line and a dramatic peaked skylight visible from the bottom of the driveway. The rest of the house comes into view as you drive up the steep approach between rock outcroppings and trees.

Making sunlight your friend. A ridge monitor fills the interior with a soft, indirect luminosity. Lower windows are fully protected from direct sunlight.

X-ray vision. It took more than a passing look to see this fabulous house site buried beneath the overgrowth and rock ledge.

Fresh air to clear the mind. Three interior windows bring better ventilation and more light to this home office. And they make it easier to place an order for lunch from the kitchen below.

Homeowner's Journal

❝ I kept telling them I wanted something simple; even starkly simple. ❞

What Mollie Byrnes appreciated was the power of symmetry, proportion, and material choice in making a beautiful backdrop for the drama of daily life. With little to distract the eye, we now see that windows are perfectly centered, that the top of the window opening is lined up with the top of the cabinets and the tile splash with the bottom, and that the stainless appliances match the stainless-steel pulls. A stage free of clutter highlights the essentials.

As they discussed the project, Mollie produced a clip book of magazine articles on barns and lofts and told Paul she wanted something small, well detailed, and extremely simple. However, the plans that Paul returned with were not a literal translation of what Mollie had outlined. In fact, she suspects the clippings were largely disregarded. Yet the final design pleased both Mollie and John far more than anything they had seen in a magazine. Paul grasped the essentials of what his clients wanted and then helped them toward an expanded vision, elevating their plans from imitative to original.

Little Big House

At 6 ft. 3 in. tall and with two equally stratospheric sons, John doesn't have much trouble explaining how the original design of 2,700 sq. ft. eventually grew to 3,400 sq. ft. "We're just big people," he says. Ceilings are high and doors are oversized. The house is still somewhat smaller than the condo where they had lived, yet thanks to Paul it seems perfectly in scale with the lot.

Privacy without a gate. Because of the way the house is placed on the site, the road below disappears by the time you're halfway up the driveway. A protected site also allows the use of oversized windows without sacrificing privacy.

Making a large house appear small is a trademark of this architectural firm. Paul explains that it's all in the roof. The right pitch combined with generous overhangs can perform miracles. Besides shedding rain and snow, the overhanging roof leads the eye down and helps to ground the building solidly on its site. In the living room, the vaulted ceiling descends dramatically. Wide roof overhangs, clearly visible through a band of south-facing windows at the top of the wall, become an extension of the ceiling. The effect is powerful, drawing the eye out and down and minimizing the barrier between inside and out.

Open Plan

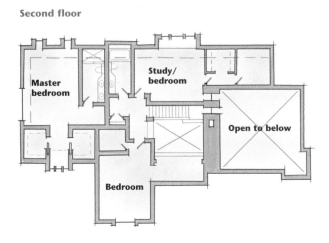

Second floor

Master bedroom

Study/bedroom

Open to below

Bedroom

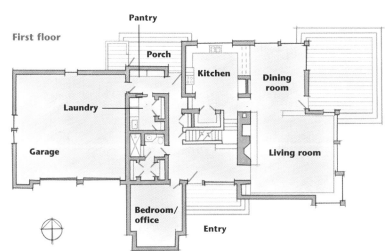

First floor

Pantry

Porch

Kitchen

Dining room

Laundry

Garage

Living room

Bedroom/office

Entry

Weathering the weather. Unless you're perfecting your tan, the south side of a house benefits from ample shade. And on rainy days, a high porch roof provides an open, outdoor experience without the worry of getting soaked.

Frames for flowers. These oversized, wraparound windows barely seem able to keep luxuriant plant life from taking over the living room.

Family-sized window seat. It's the perfect place to have that morning cup of coffee or to roll out a couple of sleeping bags for grandchildren who want to sleep under the stars. The window seat's cantilevered design also moves it past the wall line; sit here and you have the sense you're more outside than in.

Paul chose the corner of the window wall to satisfy another of Mollie's requests—a wide window seat. Because it is cantilevered beyond the wall line and into the garden, the sitting area offers a unique perspective. You are both closer to the garden and able to look back at the house, encouraging the sensation that you are sitting outside, not in the living room.

Windows are all important in connecting interior spaces with the surrounding landscape. Mollie's interest in this important detail comes naturally from her passion for sunlight and good ventilation. She thought there should be at least two windows in every room and that windows should be designed to be opened even when it rains, a not so uncommon condition along the coast. Roof overhangs protect first-floor windows, but Paul had to come up with a unique gable design to shelter dormer windows in such weather. Mollie's two-windows-per-room edict sometimes called for interior windows, such as those opening a second-floor office to the top of the stair hall and those overlooking the living room.

Form follows function. The hooded dormers that give this house so much of its character were the result of Mollie's request that all windows be operable in rainy weather. Wide roof overhangs and sidewall extensions keep rain out while complementing eaves detailing on other parts of the house.

Active entry foyer. Besides providing visual interest, an angled stair rail and interior windows in the entryway also suggest there is life and activity throughout the house.

A Celebration of Contrasts

Eliminating moldings, trim, and ornament accentuates the intrinsic beauty of the materials themselves. This ebonized cherry mantel makes a striking contrast to the cherry veneer panels that conceal the media equipment. Similarly, the manufactured quality of the stainless steel, beautiful in itself, further highlights the organic quality of the wood. The finely stuccoed hearth surround is appropriate for a fireplace, while its neutral tone and heavy masonry feel work effectively with other materials. Margins, or *reveals*, required around the panel doors have become part of the composition's vocabulary.

Help from the Homeowners

Although an extensive art collection is John's most personal expression in this house, he does claim one specific design victory as his alone—the dining-room lamps. John acquired the hand-blown vases for "a song." Fitted with lamps, the three pendants make a striking counterpoint to the clean, simple lines of the interior.

Remember Mollie's request for a design that was small, well detailed, and simple? On more than one occasion, she had to keep her designers on track. "Originally, all this was much more complicated and fancy," she says of the kitchen and dining room, "so I had to redesign the whole thing." The layout wasn't altered much, but detailing and finishes were dramatically simplified. Using a renowned cabinet shop, Kochman, Reidt, and Haigh, everything was distilled to its simplest form. The intent was to make an uncluttered backdrop for the couple's art and glass collections, but there was an unexpected bonus. The simple design brought the flawless old-world craftsmanship of the cabinetry to center stage and made it part of the display.

Simple dining elegance.
Although the dining area is casual and open, the clean lines of the built-ins combined with the Byrneses' artful furnishings create a sophisticated ambiance. The three overhead lights are adapted from hand-blown vases.

An unusual fireplace mantel and stair railing are two other essential interior details where inspired collaboration played a part. The ebonized cherry and stainless-steel mantel had already been built by the time the stair railing became an issue. The stairs grab the spotlight immediately as soon as you pass through the huge front door. Paul let the design brew until the very last moment. Mollie, ever protective of her simplified aesthetic, suggested the stairs be composed from the same palette of materials used in the fireplace mantel. After several designs were prepared, Mollie finally chose one with an unusual arrangement of angular shapes—straightforward but hardly plain.

Paul claims this is one of the few houses for which he has no misgivings. Asked if there is any part of it he would explore further in future houses, he smiles and says, "I think the ideas we developed around the stairs could be taken a lot further." Great collaborators never sleep.

Dining room flair in the kitchen. A display of bowls elevates a functional pass-through to stylish divider, helping to keep rooms separate while maintaining efficient access.

A STATEMENT WITH STAIRS

This striking stair design uses only the most basic parts—treads, risers, balusters, and rail—but combines materials in an unexpected way, making a dramatic visual impact on visitors as soon as they come through the front door. The stair rail and the kneewall that supports it, normally parallel lines, are angled to create an upward-pointing arrow and an inherent sense of movement. From above, the angled kneewall makes a downward-pointing arrow. Stainless-steel balusters are shorter at the top than at the bottom, suggesting a scale of musical notes or even a xylophone. The potential variations on this stair are endless, leaving architect MacNeely with plenty of plans for additional exploration in future houses.

WHEN IS THE HEARTH NOT the heart of a home? When it competes with a television set wired for cable, Game Boy®, and Pay-Per-View®. In the same way, even a panoramic vista may suffer second billing when weighed against today's sprawling entertainment centers. Increasingly, designers and homeowners must wrestle with these competing interests as they consider room size and furniture layout. Their solutions are as varied as the homes and homeowners, but there seem to be two basic approaches.

The owners of this Chicago house located a fireplace in their principal social space (right), choosing to use a windowless room below grade to simulate the true ambiance of a movie house (below).

In the city, where space is at a premium and views are rare, both television and hearth are often accommodated in the same room with a right-angle furniture layout that allows both to be enjoyed.

An approach that accommodates both the television and the hearth in the same space is the most popular and most affordable. This requires just a bit more room for a furniture layout that allows people to enjoy both the hearth (or the view) and the television. Since television is acoustical as well as visual, this assumes that everyone in the room will be able

Initially, the master bedroom in this Seattle home was blessed with "only" a nice hearth and a spectacular view. Subsequent advances in thin-screen technology allowed the addition of a television, making the visual menu rich indeed.

to agree on what they want to be doing at any given point. It's also necessary to address the aesthetics of the equipment even when it's not in use. A huge monitor and other components plus stacks of CDs and videocassettes are a distraction if not properly housed.

A more expansive approach allocates a separate room for multimedia entertainment, whether it's a little television set or an entire home theater. Such media rooms can fit nicely into those windowless areas that otherwise might be wasted space. Separate rooms allow dedicated furniture layouts, and everyone gets to enjoy what they like.

Once again, clever design overcomes space limitations. This elegant hearth design effortlessly morphs into a full-featured entertainment center.

Drama and Innovation

In the inner thoughts of most people building a new house, there's a worried little voice

that warns, "This is the most expensive undertaking of your whole life—play it safe." Henry Kahle

and Ian Nabashima, however, seemed to hear a characteristically different voice. "This is a once-in-a-

lifetime opportunity," it seemed to say. "Take a chance on art. Risk innovation. See the whole affair as

human drama." Indeed, the stage was already set for drama—a tragedy, it seemed.

New spaces create new possibilities. While a house must
provide for the occupants' known needs, a good design may
also provide the potential for hitherto unrealized activities—
as in the case of this window seat at the top of the stairs.

Henry and Ian were among thousands made homeless by the Oakland fire of 1991. Their tiny lot at the end of a cul-de-sac, right next to a California freeway, was nothing but scorched earth. They had lost everything. Nevertheless, these quiet gentlemen, students of theater and the arts for more than three decades, understood the blackened earth was also a blank canvas. Their loss offered a unique opportunity to both create a new home and embark on an unusual creative collaboration.

Metaphor for a new house. Made homeless by a devastating fire, the homeowners approached reconstruction with a sense of adventure. A metal sculpture of a futuristic spaceship hanging over the stairway is emblematic of their ability to face the unknown with courage.

Auditioning Architects: The Garbage Can Test

Instinctively, Ian understood that they needed an architect. But how, he wondered, could they afford one when they barely had enough money for building materials? After a few discouraging interviews, a friend's daughter suggested Karl Wanaselja, a recent graduate of the University of California at Berkeley. Although young and unlicensed, Wanaselja had been in the building trades for more than 10 years. Just as important, Ian recalls, the watercolors in his office stairway revealed an artist's eye. The audition was promising.

Ian was clear about what they wanted. He told Wanaselja the design must be innovative, even flighty, and full of light. He wanted a balcony off his bedroom and a secret passageway like Batman's. Henry favored an atrium plan with seamless access to the garden. And they both wanted a place for the car that didn't look like a place for the car.

As is the case with many young designers, Wanaselja was motivated by environmental concerns. He proposed a solar structure built from recycled and sustainable materials. To promote his idea, he quickly turned out dozens of design

The lot shapes the house. Architect Karl Wanaselja's first task was to fit the new house to a lot that was hemmed in on one side by a highway and limited by tight property-line setbacks. He managed to make this city house feel like it's in the country.

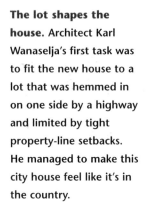

It is the little things. Counterbalanced with a rock, this ingenious front gate swings open with only a fingers' touch

alternatives and several models. Henry was overwhelmed. Ian was delighted.

Although they both admired Wanaselja's enthusiasm, they also worried that their young architect might know little about the ordinary details that make a house truly livable—storage, bathrooms, and kitchen layout. So they devised a test, challenging Wanaselja to solve the most pedestrian problem they could think of: Find a way to keep the garbage cans convenient to the front gate but out of sight. Although trivial in the context of the whole house, Wanaselja's solution was so clever Henry and Ian became convinced that any well-stated problem would receive a similarly inspired response. On one side of a fence separating the garden from the street, Wanaselja built an enclosure for the garbage cans, using the same materials as the fence to blend them visually. When trash collectors show up, they open doors on the street side of the fence to retrieve the cans. Wanaselja's solution keeps the cans completely out of sight from either side.

Homeowner's Journal

" This sliding bookcase allows me to close off my bedroom from the rest of the house in a better way than just using an everyday door. It's a concession to my idiosyncrasies and my wildest dreams. I'm quirky about English mysteries, and I've always liked the idea of a room behind a bookcase. My architect was clever enough to figure this out when I asked for a secret passage, like Batman's. "

Protect your design. A skylight that illuminates a concrete wall and stairway is curved to match the shape of the wall. Although the architect offered to take the skylight out of the plans to save money, the homeowners told him this detail outweighed any potential savings.

An Improvisation in Several Acts

The basic shape of the house evolved from three conditions: the freeway to the south, the tight boundary setbacks, and the lot's orientation to the sun's line of travel. Wanaselja sited the house as far west on the site as possible to make the most of the morning sun. He gave the rest of the property over to a patio and garden. The proximity of the freeway meant the south wall of the house would be mostly solid to block as much noise as possible, with a gentle curve matching the contour of the lot line and the highway. The wall and staircase that run along it are illuminated by a curved skylight above. To the east, the floor plan opens to the patio and garden, which is contained and protected by a carport disguised as a trellised garden shed. In an imaginative use of unconventional building materials, Wanaselja used garage doors to open part of the house to an adjoining garden area.

Tight Site

Second floor

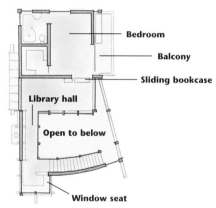

- Bedroom
- Balcony
- Sliding bookcase
- Library hall
- Open to below
- Window seat

First floor

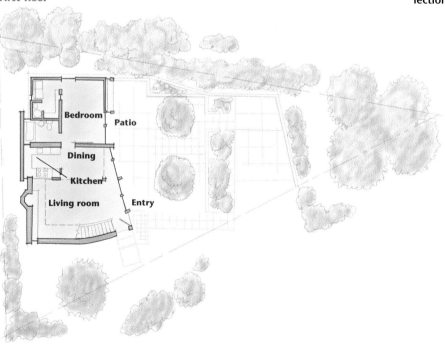

- Bedroom
- Patio
- Dining
- Kitchen
- Living room
- Entry

Reinventing the best from the past. This beautiful chain downspout is an idea that goes back to pre-Colonial Europe when rainwater was a resource too important to waste. Unlike a conventional downspout, a chain directs water precisely to a collection barrel without splashing.

The many faces of concrete.
In choosing concrete as a primary material for both walls and floors, Wanaselja was able to vary surface textures from very smooth to textured and rough. Concrete could also serve as its own finish without any additional wall or floor coverings.

Walls that move out of the way. Cheap and functional, these garage doors open to connect the garden and the open, two-story portion of the house, giving a whole new meaning to that architectural adage to "bring the outdoors inside."

Contrast catches the eye.
The architect creates visual
delight by adding a finely finished shelf to the rugged horizontal texture of the walls.

Wanaselja specified concrete for walls and floors, at the
time an unconventional idea that had several advantages.
Concrete can be its own finish surface, meaning that walls
and floors made of concrete do not have to be covered with
additional building materials. Concrete can be cast in any
color and any finish, from brutally rough to baby-skin
smooth. Its high mass neutralizes highway noise even as it
moderates heat gain from windows. Radiant-floor heat—a
network of hot-water lines buried in the concrete floor—
eliminates the need for conventional baseboard radiators. A
final bonus was that the boards used to form walls could be
recycled and used to make trellises and retaining walls outside.

Wanaselja's plan for reconstruction was sound. But Ian
and Henry's open-minded sense of adventure about their
new house and Wanaselja's decision to gather his building
crew mostly from the ranks of architecture students also
opened the door to architectural improvisation that otherwise might not have been possible.

Stepping Up

When Ian asked how he was supposed to climb
into his built-in bathtub without a step, Karl
smiled and disappeared outside. He returned

with a beautiful rock that
he had set aside as the
site was being excavated.
With Ian looking on, Karl
placed the rock where it
could be both a step and
a part of the décor. With
Ian's approval, the rock
was mortared in perma-
nently. This kind of serendipity is possible only
when the architect also happens to be the
foreman of the crew.

Musical light switches. So much more interesting
than a bland bank of four switches, this detail was the
result of playful improvisation by a team of designer-
builders. The pattern also has a practical advantage: It
made it much easier for the homeowners to remember
what each switch controlled.

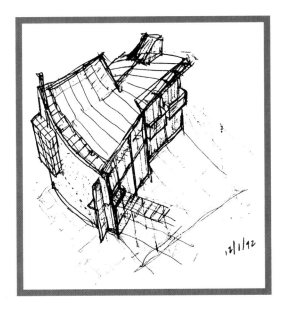

USING YOUNG ARCHITECTS

For those who don't think they can afford an experienced architect, Ian Nabashima and Henry Kahle have a suggestion: Consider a recent architectural graduate or even a student. What Karl Wanaselja lacked in professional design experience was more than outweighed by his energy, imagination, and creativity. The fact that Karl also had years of practical building experience behind him was another plus, as was his willingness to enlist the help of architectural students and turn them into a construction crew. For Ian and Henry, there was the additional comfort of knowing that Wanaselja's design had received the Honor Award for Design from the local chapter of the American Institute of Architects.

A Script with Great Dialogue

The best architecture comes from a healthy give and take between client, architect, and builder. Some of what the clients gave, Wanaselja wasn't so eager to take. Wanaselja, for example, hadn't included a balcony in his original plans, even though Ian had been clear that he wanted one. He hadn't forgotten about it, but he was looking for a minimal, sculptural shape to the building, and he feared the balcony and its awning would interfere. Put it back in the plans, Ian told him. Wanaselja complied but pushed for the same open railing used elsewhere on the house instead of the visually opaque railing Ian had requested. In the end, Ian stood firm, insisting on both the balcony and a canvas railing. Today, Wanaselja concedes the canvas looks great with the matching awnings.

Open your mind to different material choices. Canvas is used here to integrate the patio (umbrella) and balcony (railing) with the roof (awnings). Less expensive than conventional detailing, the canvas becomes an important part of the material palette for the house rather than looking like an afterthought.

The delight of a surprise. This wall niche was never on a drawing or even discussed. Then one day the owners came home and there it was. The niche makes a perfect home for a special vase and helps define the area visually as the dining room.

Cast in place. Because the architect personally formed and poured the concrete walls, they were carefully detailed to incorporate recessed doors, lighting, and other design features.

In deliberations over the hearth, Wanaselja was more convincing. Ian and Henry felt they couldn't justify the expense of a fireplace that would get only infrequent use. But in this open floor plan, Wanaselja explained, a fireplace served a critical function in helping to define the living room. It was part of the design's "functional zoning" in which spaces are defined not by walls but by use and visual clues, such as varying ceiling heights and wall treatments—and fireplaces. The hearth was saved.

Walls, where they do occur, are never just blank dividers. Rather, they incorporate sliding doors, built-in shelves, niches, and other spontaneous design details. Many of these visual delights came from a sudden inspiration on the part of the designer-builders, who saw possibilities during construction and, with tools in hand, acted on them. Some, inevitably, were just out-and-out surprises, like the day Henry came home to find a large window seat at the top of the stairs. It was, Ian told him, his new sewing room.

A Star Production

Humble materials and a tiny site notwithstanding, the crucial ingredient in this project was the special blend of players. A young architect overflowing with ideas and idealism, more interested in getting built than getting rich, found clients who appreciated innovation and remained open to any idea that didn't break the bank. More than 10 years later, Henry and Ian are still thrilled with the results, and Wanaselja knows this may be the most inspired house of his career.

A hearthless house is a heartless house. While fires are seldom needed in Oakland, California, imagine what this wall would look like without the fireplace. Although the homeowners weren't sure it was necessary, the architect knew it would play a crucial role in defining interior spaces, what he calls "functional zoning."

Getting There

While most people keep second homes to get away, Crystal Liston created this coastline

beauty hoping to get back—back to something she'd had long before. From the start, Crystal saw this

beach cabin as a place where friends and family would gather for a few days of fun and relaxation.

Wheelchair-bound since an auto accident in her teens, Crystal may also have found a way to recon-

struct the warmth of her childhood, a time when her parents were still married, when her mother told

stories of her own childhood summers on the beach, and before Crystal began her life on wheels.

Leave your dress clothes behind. Beach cabin architecture, like
the lifestyle it sustains, is an informal affair. This box derives its
character from a spirited use of materials, a butterfly roof, and the
owner's eclectic collection of curios.

Front-row seats. Although Crystal had imagined the house at water's edge, conservation covenants kept it well back from the shore. An unexpected dividend was a sweeping view of wind-ruffled dune grass and sky.

Better than stairs. When properly designed, a ramp will always be more appealing than stairs. A leisurely stroll up or down is perfectly consistent with beach life.

Proper porthole placement. The porthole allows bathers to see out but also allows others to see in. Since Crystal's house is the only one out here, this is not a problem.

Crystal began keeping her eye open for affordable shorefront property where she could build. When she heard about land that seemed suitable in Ocean Shores, Washington, she grabbed a real estate agent and made the 2½-hour trip to take a look. So began a journey that by her own estimation has completely changed her life.

A Secret Plan

Crystal had her reasons for keeping the project a secret until it was entirely finished. Relying solely on the advice of the real estate agent, she'd purchased a lot where she thought she would be able to build at water's edge. Only later did Geoff Prentiss, the architect she'd hired to design the house, explain that zoning setbacks would prevent her from building right on the water. It was more likely that she would actually see the water only from the second floor. It was a challenge Prentiss was happy to accept.

He placed all the living spaces on the second floor, including a sweeping deck and hot tub. Access to the upper part of the house is by a regal ramp. No mere code requirement, the ramp makes a celebration of gaining the necessary height to embrace an ocean view. At grade, the house makes friends with an equally beautiful view of the moors.

Assuming she would be getting something like a log cabin, Crystal was surprised at what Prentiss designed. She was also thrilled. The simple shape of the building and its butterfly roof give the appearance that the house is scanning the western horizon. This is a beach cabin as optimistic and interesting as its owner.

Eclectic Epiphany

While Geoff deserves full credit for his clever solution to the architectural puzzle represented by this project, Crystal's collaboration was crucial to the whimsy of the finished spaces. In addition to capturing the mood of her mother's beach stories, Crystal also wanted some reference to a little cabin her father had built in the Alaska hinterlands. There were also objects she wanted to incorporate into the design that represented favorites memories—a tugboat door, a few portholes, some wainscoting, and a pressed-tin ceiling. Colors and finishes were discussed and debated, but the final choices were hers.

Exuberant color transforms everyday walls. Crystal's choice of vibrant colors enlivens her beachside house even on dreary days. Although she discussed finishes and colors with her architect, ultimately she picked what she liked.

ARCHITECT'S CORNER

THE LANGUAGE OF A ROOF

The shape of a roof can impart a protected air to a house, as if the roof were enfolding the house and keeping its occupants safe. But a roof can say something else entirely. This "butterfly" roof that Geoff Prentiss designed for Crystal Liston's beach house is sculpturally more about lightness of spirit and forward-looking optimism than it is about seeking shelter. The upside-down roof form, which dates back to at least the 1940s, implies the dancing motion of a butterfly or bird, and it goes straight to the heart of the project. "The goal," says Geoff, "was to make a fun, idiosyncratic playhouse with eclectic features while keeping it all easily accessible for someone who lives on wheels."

A rare scene. Family and friends come here to relax, but the ambiance in this house is seldom subdued. In truth, Crystal and her guests are a young, active crew, and this house sees a lot of playtime.

This energetic young woman, always inclined to see the glass half full instead of half empty, hadn't spent much time wondering how the house would accommodate wheelchair living. Prentiss, in fact, seemed more concerned than she was. She worried that by lowering counters, windows, and sinks, she would make the house awkward for her family and friends. She was so used to dealing with an uncooperative environment that it hardly occurred to her that there might be an alternative. Prentiss had to remind her repeatedly that it was to be *her* house and should be designed for her lifestyle.

Beyond the ramp to the second-floor deck, there are a few concessions to Crystal's use of a wheelchair. Counter heights are lower, for example, and Prentiss included a wheelchair-sized elevator that ascends from the garage area to the main floor of the house.

Beach Cabin

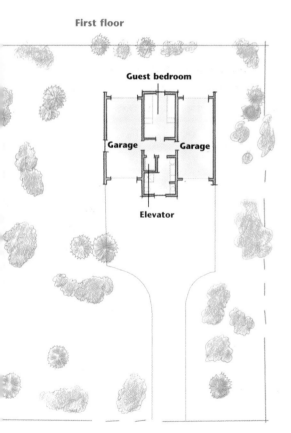

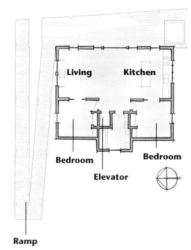

Little changes, big effects. Simply by lowering the counters and rehinging cabinet doors, architect Geoff Prentiss perfectly customized this kitchen to Crystal's life on wheels.

Dollhouse scale shift. Lowered counters, cabinets, and coat hooks suggest a huge volume of space, but the standard-size stools tell a different story. The shift in such reference points gives this great living room a cozy, human scale.

Custom Character

For the kitchen counter, Crystal wanted something special. She had some Japanese fishing buoys that she thought would look good with a copper countertop. Prentiss introduced her to Karl, an old-world woodworker, and together they fashioned this joyful jazz of materials into a very personal creation. It probably goes without saying that the buoys conceal electric lights that can be dimmed.

The Proof Is in the Playing

Crystal furnished this modern piece of architecture with secondhand furniture and a few purchases from Ikea®. Sharing a place with friends inevitably means a certain amount of breakage, and she didn't want the furnishings to get in the way of the main purpose of the place—to have fun.

When the house is full, Crystal gives the master bedroom over to guests and sleeps on the couch. She doesn't consider this a sacrifice. After all, she'll get the first view of the morning sun. Double pocket doors that close off her bedroom can be opened to connect the two upstairs bedrooms to the main living room when she entertains really large groups. On the first floor there's a commodious bunkroom for her many friends. Twin garage spaces have automatic doors at each end, allowing an uninterrupted view through the building to the dune grass on the other side. What might have been an unattractive, utilitarian space is completely engaged with its surroundings. It's a wonderful setting for after-dark and rainy-day activities.

Tricky transoms. It's not easy to get the right tilt and proportions for an angled window in an orthogonal design. Practiced restraint and skillful use of materials makes this challenging composition look easy.

Memories from Alaska. For Crystal, huge slabs of spruce fill the bedroom with smells and memories of her father's cabin in Alaska. Double doors treat late risers to the living room's ocean view.

No match for a clam bake. Maybe not, but when the weather turns foul and the guests include a handful of kids, this indoor/outdoor area becomes a welcome recreation space. Doors that open at both ends of the garage space make the most of the scenery that lies beyond.

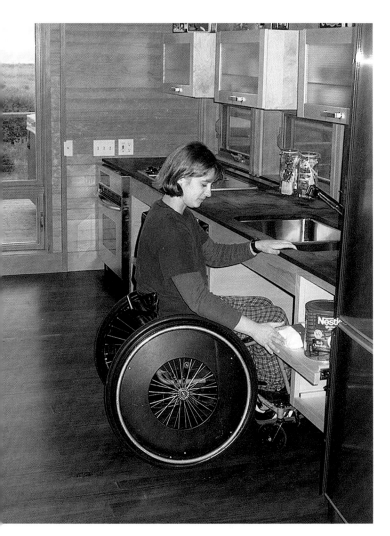

Inspiration is a human quality. The shape of our homes is inspired by the shape of our lives. Crystal's passion for life, family, and friends is embossed into every inch of this spirited beach house.

Although the house is designed for different-size groups and varied occasions, it seems there's no upstaging the view. Even in winter, with the wind howling and dune grass bent flat, house guests collect on the deck or in the hot tub, mesmerized by the show of nature.

A Secret Unveiled

As the house took shape, Crystal kept her secret. But when it was completed, it was time for an unveiling. Crystal made a date with her mother to go for a ride, "to see a secret," she explained. Her mother allowed herself to be blindfolded and bundled into the car for the long drive from Seattle to the beach. When they arrived, Crystal took her mother, still wearing a blindfold, upstairs and sat her in a chair facing the view. Playing to her mother's love of science fiction and drama, Crystal flipped on her sound system. As *Also Sprach Zarathustra*, the dramatic opening salvo of *2001, A Space Odyssey*, flooded the room and the electrically operated storm shutters rolled back to reveal the view, Crystal removed the blindfold. Her three-year secret was revealed.

For Crystal, the project was emotionally and physically exhausting. Nevertheless, she says it was one of the most amazing experiences of her life, and there may well be another house somewhere in her future. Her advice for anyone contemplating such an adventure? "Be firm," she says, "and stay true to yourself." A most concise formula for any inspired house.

One Final Move

Terri and Geoff Fletcher agreed they could handle one last move. Searching for a small

place comfortably situated in its surroundings, the Fletchers became house-tour regulars from their

home in Austin, Texas. Perhaps the house they finally found on Vashon Island, Washington, was

also searching for them. It had been moved twice before it was finally placed on the concrete foun-

dation where they came across it. By then, the boxy ranch was badly run down, looking unloved

and adrift.

Framing the view without frustrating the viewer. View, space,
and living flow in and out with minimum interference from a
cleanly detailed design that includes generous use of glass, decks,
and cable railings.

It didn't matter to Geoff. Standing on its dilapidated deck, he was mesmerized by the view of Puget Sound and the Olympic Mountains. But Terri, a painter and fabric artist, just couldn't get past how grim the house looked. Noting her distress, the real estate agent handling the sale introduced them to local architect David Brown. The Fletchers and David immediately clicked, and the deal was sealed. Before returning to their home in Texas, the Fletchers gave him a description of what they wanted in their new home. There was no love lost on the existing structure, but neither could they afford to start from scratch. Or so they thought.

Fitting in. Staggered shapes that create deep shadows help to keep the house from resembling a big brick. The constellation of glass, wood, and roofing is seen as a collection of visual events rather than as one simple shape. The active façade harmonizes with the woods, following the same visual principles.

Split-level entry. Trying to connect the driveway directly to the upper level would have resulted in too many steps. This elegant solution gives equal access to both floors.

Reconnecting House and Site

David studied the Fletchers' wish list. They had asked him to modify the house so that it didn't look as though it had been placed there by a roll of the dice. They dreamed of a home so well sited and so sensitively configured that every room would be suffused with the beauty of the surrounding landscape. They wanted it finished in regional materials, with a simple shape, and made to look as if it belonged there. The Fletchers do not have children, but they have lots of cats, like to entertain, and needed enough room for two home-based occupations. With an unrepressed sunlight habit developed in the South, they asked David for a design that collected every beam and ray the Northwestern sky might offer.

After careful analysis of what the Fletchers wanted and what he had to work with, David decided that even saving the foundation would be a challenge. As a result, the only vestige of the original structure is the footprint on which the new house was built.

SOME HOUSES SHOULDN'T BE SAVED

Buildings that have been around for a while are almost always out of square, out of plumb, or both, and they usually come with mechanical and material problems that are waiting to be discovered. Unless the house is a historic property, it's often less expensive and less time-consuming to demolish a questionable structure rather than work around its shortcomings. The question really becomes, what of value will be lost by tearing it down? In the case of this house, which was originally located at a local airport, then hauled across town before being dropped on a concrete foundation, there wasn't much worth saving.

While the house is simple on the inside, the new design uses varied rooflines and an active façade to break down the scale of the exterior, which helps it blend in with the woodlands behind. A split-level entry brings guests into the house midway between the work areas on the lower level and the living spaces on top. By minimizing the number of steps before entering, the house has a more comfortable connection with its surroundings. The hammered concrete walls that run along the steps are an imaginative way to suggest there was another building on the site before this one.

Inside, a gallery hall leads dramatically to a full-house panorama where floor-to-ceiling windows and decks on all sides create an almost explosive feeling of space. By minimizing window mullions, casings, and other trim, David reduced architectural distractions that would inhibit visual flow. This subtle strategy helps the eye move outside of the building to take in the landscape—intimate views to the east, sweeping views to the west. Similarly, the kitchen counter is designed without a backsplash so the surface seems to continue right through the window, taking your eye along for the ride.

Artwork entry. From the foyer, galleries on both levels are immediately apparent, and the entire layout of the house becomes clear. The slight angle between levels is all that's needed to avoid the stacked feel of a cheap motel.

Contrast makes it wonderful. These nicely detailed railings are more attractive than most for outside decks, but on the interior they are even more striking. The contrast with the finished wood makes both materials stand out.

Facing the View

Main floor

Laundry

Television room

Entry

Covered entry walk

Gallery

Covered deck

Master bedroom

Living room

Dining

Kitchen

Deck

Covered deck

Gallery living. The upper level is one large room with functional areas defined by ceiling heights, floor finishes, and the layout of furniture. Objects and furniture almost seem to float in the flow of space.

A still body of water? Without a backsplash or sill to interfere, the kitchen counter looks like a beautiful green liquor running out and over the window edge.

Second place is pretty good. When the view is this majestic, the prudent architect knows better than to compete. Making it easy to see outside and keeping details clean bring the power of place into the very heart of the home.

Resonance in Design

Using similar materials, treatments, and details inside and out brings coherence to a design. For example, the hammered edges of concrete walls at the entry reappear as the rusticated edge of granite sills inside. The granite surround shown here was meant to be in the shape of south Texas. The rough tooling recalls the concrete at the entry, even if the shape is less successful at recalling the state (El Paso fell off in the carving). These kinds of treatments may not be obvious at first, but ultimately they are what give the design depth and richness.

Architecture gains coherence when materials and methods used on the exterior can also be applied on the interior. David's design, for example, called for railings made of thin cable because it doesn't interfere with the sense of space. He used cable railings inside and outside and found a way to use exposed cable for some interior lights and in the construction of hearth-side shelves. In the same way, he duplicated the rustic quality of the front steps in the edge treatment of granite in the bathrooms and in the gallery. Using the same materials and details throughout the house subliminally blurs the distinction between inside and outside spaces. And if this detailing and the views aren't enough, every room has a door to the outside, including the laundry room.

Sleeping in the treetops. There's little space in this room for anything more than the bed and the view but that's all it takes, claim the Fletchers, to get every day off to a good start.

Meanwhile, Back in Texas

It's never easy to design and build a house while the owners are half a nation away. It's all too easy for owners to fall out of synch with the project. With the best of intentions, they can make suggestions that are hard to incorporate. For David, this challenge presented itself in the form of an ornate hand-carved Indonesian transom that Terri found in the back room of an Austin import shop. Not that David wasn't used to accommodating special objects on this job: Every niche in the gallery was specifically made for a particular piece of art. But this one just seemed wrong for the lean, airy design he was trying to create. Yet once installed, the transom created just the right contrast with the minimalist aesthetic in the rest of the house. David decided that if the overall design truly reflected his clients' taste, it could accommodate their whimsy as well. Houses, like people, are rarely 100% consistent.

Art galleries don't need gravity. These cable-supported shelves, like similarly supported kitchen counters and stairs, appear to float in thin air, redirecting our attention to the space between objects and freeing us to imagine a gravity-free world of art.

A tough room to work. The television room off the main living space may have trouble keeping an audience. Like every room in the house, it has a door to the outside, and that's a hard act to follow.

66 Architectural design involves more than the general layout of the house and the pitch of the roof. It's also about floor styles and niches, cabinet knobs and toilet-paper holders. It is intimate and personal. Find an architect who listens, who shares your sense of style, and most important, is someone you are comfortable with. **99**

—Terri and Geoff Fletcher

The transom, some lights, and a couple of sinks are Texas treasures that help Terri and Geoff stay connected with their past. Each was an unexpected design change that just showed up on site. And that's where David's working relationship with his builders was so important. Because they understood what David was attempting architecturally, they could ad-lib installations to look as if they had always been part of the design.

Concentrated flourish. An ornate hand-carved transom accentuates the minimalist design of the house while marking the importance of the master bedroom doors at the end of the hall.

Finally finished. The last piece of driftwood on the Fletcher site was an old tool shed that was dragged out of the woods to the edge of the new vegetable garden.

Long-View Landscaping

The best residential architecture never separates building from grounds; to improve either requires changes to both. Michael Lee, the landscape architect on this project, was kept plenty busy regrading and planting the property. He used beautiful native grasses to give the feeling that the landscape had been there before the building. In the very last phase of the project, Lee's crew dragged an abandoned utility building out of the woods and set it up as a garden shed. With a new roof and siding, it looks as if it's always been there. Like the homeowners and their new home, it's there for good.

Queen of the Corner

In any package deal, the buyer inevitably ends up with some junk along with the good stuff.

Nevertheless, Cris Wasiak, a banker with a design degree in her back pocket, knew that the derelict

property in Baltimore's Federal Hill district was a gold mine. Of the three separate buildings stepping

up the road, two had been torn down and rebuilt during a road rebuilding project in the 1920s and

the third dated from the early 19th century. All were far past their prime and had yet to be united

into a single, coherent property.

The demands of history. Adapting a modern lifestyle to a historic house is not for everyone.
Three previous owners, frustrated with the codes and ordinances, sold without renovating:
Only like-minded residents tend to settle in historic neighborhoods.

When a historic structure acquires badly built appendages, particularly if they have become derelict, the reclamation process can be a nightmare. But Cris's undergraduate degree in architecture helped her see what others didn't. Not only did this property occupy an important corner and have a tremendous view of Baltimore's Inner Harbor, but it also came with architect Becky Swanston. Becky had stayed with these buildings through two previous owners, the last exhausted and disheartened by a zoning battle with the local preservation society. With Becky's help, Cris would see the project through, and her corner would eventually become a center for neighborhood social activity.

Fitting into the Neighborhood

Cris and Becky formed a remarkable design team, collaborating on the overall design but also showing individual strengths. Becky, who had served on the Historical Preservation Society and lived in Federal Hill for 21 years, was the perfect architect for the formidable task of unifying the building's varied parts. Cris stayed busy chasing down bathroom fixtures, tile, lighting, knobs, and other hardware, right down to special screws for the railings. "Having a client like Cris allowed me to immediately raise the design process to the next level," says Becky, "because she understood the whole project."

Becky, highly respected for her work on Federal Hill, has a reputation for thoughtfully combining new and old. A long-sought zoning variance for Cris's property allowed her to remove the worthless post-1920s structures, but her replacement designs met with endless review. She argued that the façade on Montgomery Avenue, the main street, should be restored in the same fashion as the rest of that historic street. But on the less-traveled Williams Street side, she felt a more contemporary treatment would let in more light, provide garage space, and "celebrate" the corner. This inspired idea endured 11 plan revisions before eventually gaining approval.

While the municipality was giving Becky a hard run on the outside, Cris had an equally daunting set of goals for the inside.

MARRYING OLD AND NEW

Overlapping and sometimes contradictory guidelines can make the rebuilding of historic buildings a challenge. For architect Becky Swanston, reconstructing three adjoining properties in Baltimore's Federal Hill district called for plans that steered a middle course—neither literal copies of period houses nor modern designs without any feel for historical precedent.

In Becky's words, "I'm always trying to push the envelope a little because I really like the juxtaposition of new with old. A lot of people thought that this was too contemporary a solution for such a prominent corner. But I've served on the Historical Preservation Society in design review, and that's my reputation. I'm always trying to open their eyes to new things that can work in a historic context."

Rooftop luxury. Due to the city's inherent density, activities normally reserved for the backyard may be transferred to the roof. This includes socializing between neighbors. Cris and her neighbors enjoy regular roof parties and converse at length, even across the street.

The ties that bind. Part of any design should include accommodations for visiting family and friends. With an extended family in England in the habit of visiting in large numbers for weeks at a time, Cris made this consideration a paramount design objective.

Where old meets new. The level changes that often occur in historic renovations can be put to good use. The bookshelves, stairs, and lowered ceiling announce that you are entering the historic portion of the house. At the same time, the architect has defined a nice den off the living room.

Make Room for Family and Friends

Although raised in New York City, Cris has an extended family in England. Their annual visits to see her normally last for a couple of weeks and require as many as six additional beds. Combining a couple of smaller houses, with separate entries, into one well-configured domicile became the perfect solution for these family migrations. It also works well for a homeowner who likes to entertain.

Even more than the bed count, Cris was articulate about her architectural requirements: light, view, and space. This equation was easily solved on the roof, where there is an abundance of all three. Here, Becky designed a rooftop living room, complete with radiant heater, mist fan, refrigerator, and comfortable seating for more than a dozen. A seasoned city dweller, Cris is a big fan of rooftop living. She happily communes with neighbors on their roofs or in the street and invites them to join her for open-air festivities.

Historic upgrade. Built in the same location as the original stairs, this contemporary design uses similar materials and has the advantage of being code compliant.

More Than the Sum of Its Parts

Stairs and subtle changes in level are the key to combining three different buildings into one cohesive residence. The outlines of the original building seem to blur and disappear as you move from the foundation level through the second and third floors to the rooftop. Remarkably, the northern stairs remain in their original location even though they have been completely remodeled.

Master bedroom

Third floor

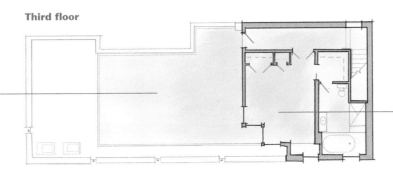

Roof deck

Second floor

Library

Kitchen

Laundry

Living room

Sitting area

Dining

Stairway

First floor

Terrace

Front entry

Garage

Study/ bedroom

Bedroom

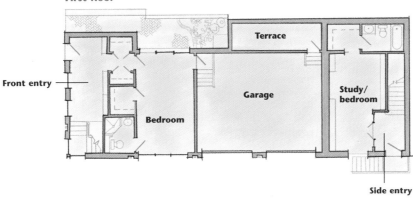

Side entry

Kitchen collection. Designed for easy socializing, this kitchen also features a small portion of Cris's extensive wine-glass collection. Additional glass pieces are displayed behind glazed cabinet doors with built-in lighting.

Perfect placement. The television is situated so it can be seen from the kitchen as well as the couch. Similarly, the fireplace is visible from all points, including the dining area. Bookshelves and collection displays have completely replaced bare walls.

The Tactile House

In every home there's a world of small-scale features where the hand comes into physical contact with the house. Often over-looked, doorknobs, window blinds, railings, light switches, and drawer pulls typify the sort of small details that establish the "feel" of a house. While bad craftsmanship can't be saved with a nice knob, the opposite is all too common—beautiful doors compromised with bad hardware. Taking the time to find quality appointments is an effort that will be repaid every time you open the door, raise the blind, turn on the light, or run your hand along the stair rail.

Knowing that Cris is a hostess who likes to cook, Becky designed an open kitchen on the middle floor that accommodates small, casual get-togethers. For grander occasions, there is a formal dining area and living room, both within conversational distance of the cook. A small window bay helps define the dining area, while a fireplace surrounded by ebonized ash anchors the living room. Cris's choices of color and appointments greatly enhance the definition of kitchen, dining, and living areas. The result is a flexible layout with character and texture that works as well for large affairs as it does for the intimate get-togethers.

Access and control. Bringing in too much sunlight is a formula for glare and overheating. Carefully designed shutters allow the light to be controlled, while patterned glass further diffuses light entering Cris's private study.

Private Spaces

Even a very social animal needs an inner sanctum, and Cris wanted one with plenty of sunlight. At the top of the stairs, just off the kitchen, Becky designed a glass room that's accessible through a pocketed sliding wall. The textured glass transmits sunlight without sacrificing any privacy. Here, she has a desk, a comfortable seating area, and her best collectibles.

Cris is a morning person, and she wanted a bedroom that would be bathed in the first rays of dawn. Becky placed the third-floor master bedroom on the southeast corner with wraparound windows. These shuttered floor-to-ceiling windows are a good example of the considerable thought given to all the glazing on this side of the house. By adjusting the shutters and the operable sections of the windows, Cris can fine-tune the amount of view, light, ventilation, and sound that comes into the house. Anything less flexible on the south side could easily lead to overheating, stale air, or excessive street noise.

Not everyone is a morning person. Cris emphatically is. Separated from the roof by a single wall, this bedroom has lots of light and great views. Shutters provide privacy at night.

Cure for the chaos. Collectors won't abide too much mess since it mutes the impact of their efforts. Shelving for this task should be simple, copious, and properly spaced. Anything else will only compete with the collectibles.

Homeowner's Journal

" It got to the point where we were actually at the forge picking out the screw heads for the stair railing—should they be Phillips head or square drive? And now I see and appreciate them every time I go up or down the stairs. "

Cris understood that anything that ended up in her field of vision would either help the overall design or compromise it. By being involved, she was able to act as an intelligent safety net for things that the architect couldn't get to.

A natural collector, Cris also is an avid reader. So Becky created shelving space in every nook and cranny. Cris likes to arrange books and collectibles into fascinating presentations or, as in the entry foyer, dedicates a shelving wall to a rotating display of art objects. Among her oldest and most popular collections are the wine glasses that take up several display cases. When she entertains, guests are encouraged to choose their glasses from any case...and use more than one if they wish.

Making a Successful Entry

In just two years, Cris has won herself an integral place in this tightly knit historic neighborhood. When the construction was finally complete, she threw a big party for all the neighbors, many of whom she had never met. Since they had all been attentively surveying every phase of this special renovation, attendance was high. Indeed, this turned out to be the beginning of strong neighborhood bonds. With every year, Cris's friendships grow deeper and more numerous, both at street level and on the roof.

Cris has lived in Chicago, Cleveland, Brussels, Naples, and New York City and undertook small renovation projects in the first two. Although she enjoys living in Baltimore tremendously, she still isn't certain it will be her last stop. If she does move again, she suspects it will be to Europe and that could indeed inspire another house. But only, she adds, if she can work again with Becky. And Becky? "I'm ready any time."

FROM SIMPLE BARN DOORS to bookcases that cleverly conceal an entry, there's something magical about an assembly that slides out of the way. Even the humble garage door enjoys something in common with the universally loved rolltop desk. Opening a sliding or pocket door requires fewer body gyrations than swinging a hinged door, so one of the great features of a pocket door is the relative composure of the person entering the room. It's almost like making a stage entrance.

Equipped with translucent "reeded" glass, this traditional double pocket door maintains bedroom privacy even as it allows the morning light to enter. When opened all the way, an adjoining sitting room is added to the suite.

For those who like an open plan but choose not to entertain in the kitchen, these repurposed barn sliders allow a sunny kitchen to be closed off once the meal is served. For informal or family occasions, they can be left open, effectively integrating the kitchen with the family room.

These double sliders, inspired by a Japanese folding screen, are affordably constructed from plywood. While the galley kitchen is hidden from the dining area, the cook can still keep an eye on a boiling pot.

Function and facility are also features of the sliding door. Early barn doors were large and heavy. The swinging version requires immense hinges, beefy door jambs, and demanding carpentry skills, while the slider is far easier to install and maintain. Moreover, in northern climates, a sliding barn door doesn't require snow removal. Even inside a house, the swing of a conventional door takes up space that is sometimes inconvenient. It can limit furniture placement or violate safety codes.

This entire glass wall slides up and out of the way on heavy-duty garage-door hardware, giving new meaning to the notion of "connecting the inside with the outside."

Carrying hundreds of books, the sliding bookshelf in the foreground opens to reveal a private bedroom with a small balcony, also accessible through a sliding door. Smaller designs particularly benefit from the spatial efficiency of sliders.

There was a time when the hardware for residential pocket doors wasn't very reliable. In combination with a hollow-core door, the overall experience was flimsy, and derailments were common. This created a bad reputation that is no longer deserved. Today, there is a generous choice of quality hardware allowing everything from a pocket door to a whole wall to slide effortlessly without risk of derailment. This has inspired inventive designers to solve some thorny problems and create some evocative entryways.

Without a conventional header or frame, this sliding door looks more like a sliding wall and disappears completely when open. The translucent glass preserves privacy in the homeowner's inner sanctum while allowing full natural illumination.

Garden Pavilions

With a 1940s ranch house in need of a complete renovation, Suzi and Steve Gilbert

approached the choice of architects the way an epicure delights in the prospect of a gourmet meal.

The menu was wonderful to peruse, but ultimately it required making a choice. More than 20 inter-

views later, they took a tour of architect Buzz Yudell's house and knew they had found their man.

What inspired the Gilberts was the way the spaces in Buzz's house flowed seamlessly into the

exterior landscape and the way the sequence of interior spaces made traffic patterns seem not only

Capitalizing on corners. Largely ignored before the renovation, the den is now the most popular spot in the house. The existing window bay was only changed at the corners, yet the new square shape transforms the feel and layout of this room.

Designing Inside and Outside Together

One of the first things that Steve and Suzi Gilbert noticed about architect Buzz Yudell's house was how successfully he had integrated inside and outside spaces. It was the exact quality they wanted in their own home. Buzz's secret is to work closely with a landscape architect so that rooms inside and adjoining spaces outside are designed simultaneously. The approach gives designers far more control in enhancing interior spaces than simply installing big windows and worrying about the views later.

comfortable but inevitable. These were exactly the qualities the Gilberts wanted in their own home.

But Buzz's house was new from the ground up. Steve, an engineer by training, had practical worries. Would the same kind of success be possible in a renovation? Suzi wondered whether they would be able to afford an architect of Buzz's stature. Even if they could, would he be interested in the project? The answer on all counts was yes, and Buzz responded with a plan that transformed a house with small, dark rooms into a series of larger, light-filled interior spaces firmly and naturally connected to the outside.

Walled refuge with a borrowed view. Although they have close neighbors on all sides, the Gilberts see only the tops of the trees on adjoining lots. Walls and landscaping keep each property private and tranquil.

Room to grow. A garage addition will allow the Gilberts to flex with any unanticipated change in their lifestyle. Meanwhile, it serves as a guest room, office, storage area, and lifeguard stand.

House for an Extended Family

Steve and Suzi, retired with children multiplying into grandchildren, entertain regularly and are active in their community. They needed a house that could accommodate social functions and the rambling activities of six grandchildren while still feeling intimate for a quiet evening at home. They also wanted something decidedly larger than the narrow, 9-ft.-wide Pullman-type kitchen they'd had in their previous home. They asked only for moderate closets and bathrooms, deciding to pass on the showy, oversized designs they saw in design magazines. Finally, although healthy and energetic, Steve and Suzi asked Buzz to create a design flexible enough to accommodate more limited mobility later in their lives by adding a room above the garage with a bathroom that could house live-in help should they ever need or want it.

Fabulous flow. The den steps down to a larger living room, which, in turn, flows out to an even more expansive front courtyard. It's a view that works in either direction.

Living in the garden. Two large window bays protrude into the lush side yard, giving the attached rooms a feeling of being in the garden. Wood doors and windows make a striking pattern against the stucco walls and the mass of the chimney.

Although constrained by budget and building codes that limited him to work within the existing footprint, Buzz was inspired by the Gilberts' appreciation of architecture and design. He sensed immediately that the interior of this ranch should be opened up, with rooms redesigned to align with similarly designed outdoor rooms. The design solution would involve strategic removal of some interior walls while adding doors and windows in some of the exterior walls.

Sitting in the Gilberts' family room as they discussed the couple's wish list, Buzz furiously doodled design ideas and sketched out alternatives. Walls shifted and rooms combined; new doors and windows framed expansive views. An array of outdoor rooms, varied in materials and size, were linked to interior spaces to coordinate traffic flow. Suzi and Steve were mesmerized as they watched the inside and the outside become a unified whole.

The front gate. Properly handled, a gate suggests promise and mystery as well as affording privacy. The Gilberts' entry gate benefits from an almost Japanese quality, surrounded by simple landscaping and a welcoming bench.

Inside Out

First floor

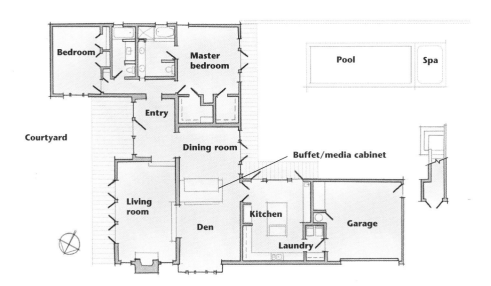

Flexible front yard. The courtyard of decomposed granite is low maintenance and can be easily set up for a large function or a smaller family affair. Without verdant landscaping on both sides, it might look more like a beach.

Kitchen with a view. A substantially enlarged kitchen easily handles a pool party for the owners' six grandchildren or a casual luncheon at the island. Best of all is a table for two with a view.

Arriving Becomes an Experience

The Gilberts' modest Los Angeles property is mostly walled and entirely surrounded by mature trees on adjoining lots. The walls and trees create a buffer between the house and its neighbors, allowing Buzz to add windows without worrying whether they would result in a loss of privacy. Buzz and landscape architect Pamela Burton worked closely together so that new windows would open views to specific features outside—trees or flower beds, for example.

The front gate opens onto a generous, almost formal, courtyard. Sensitivity to scale and detail has resulted in an area that can host large gatherings or, with slight modifications, provide a peaceful garden experience for one or two. Wraparound steps create an unobtrusive border that minimizes the inherent slope of the property and focuses attention on the front door without a lot of architectural fuss. The expanse of decomposed granite in the courtyard would seem oversized if it weren't for the plantings and a seating arrangement that creates a welcoming sense of scale. To the left, a slightly sunken pocket-garden encourages an intimate exchange with a grandchild or private meditation. Up a few steps to the right, a stunning sweep of lawn with a long bed of irises entices anyone in the living room or den.

Sink with a view. Any kitchen sink benefits from a window with a nice view. By eliminating the backsplash and minimizing window muntins, this design lightens the work by making the dishwasher feel like a part of the view.

UP REALLY CLOSE

Coherence without Drudgery

Using the same material in more than one place helps lend coherence to design. For the Gilberts' house, architect Buzz Yudell chose slate for the bathroom countertops and for an outside patio. Simply by varying its surface texture, he gives the stone many faces, gaining the advantages of consistency without allowing the look to become bland or repetitive.

Inside Becomes More of Outside

Good to his word, Buzz has referenced his home's light-filled, garden-oriented spaces in the redesign of this simple ranch. The living room space flows gracefully through six large doors to the front courtyard. Somewhat more casually, the kitchen, dining room, and master bedroom all connect with the backyard and pool area.

Interior views stretch all the way through the house to the backyard as well as diagonally through the dining area to the kitchen. Rather than making you feel as though you've entered a box, the effect is more like moving from one layer or zone into another. So much is visible and accessible that it feels like an architectural invitation to make yourself at home. Since the Gilberts entertain quite a bit, this welcoming effect suits them perfectly.

Well-ventilated welcome. The view from the front door reveals the dining room and the backyard with pool beyond. Nothing is hidden from the arriving guest.

Just add people. A comfortable arrangement of furniture in the living room, as well as several doorways that make it easy to come and go, encourage lively socializing. Carefully placed windows make the most of thoughtful landscaping outside.

Caution: For morning people only. With the bed and doorway aligned on an east-facing swimming pool, this bedroom almost feels as if it's in the backyard.

The den, most populated when children and grandchildren are visiting, coordinates perfectly with the kitchen and backyard. On a hot day, children can stay in the pool while adults supervise from the coolness of the kitchen. For large gatherings, the Gilberts make the dining room the center of activity. Guests have easy access to food from both the front and back yards and can settle comfortably in the living room, side yard, or den to eat.

Opening a house to large groups requires clear delineation of public and private spaces. Buzz sequestered the master and guest bedrooms off to the east, accessed through a small family gallery. The wall of family photos clearly announces that one is entering the private area of the house.

The only real expansion to the original house is the space that was added over the garage. Meeting many needs, this area serves as an office for Steve, a guest suite for visitors, and may someday house a health-care provider, should they want one. It adds the flexibility needed to ensure that this continues to be Suzi and Steve's ultimate home.

An Ongoing Sense of Wonder

Living in a house designed by a renowned architect expressly for their lifestyle is a kind of nirvana for Suzi and Steve. If money were no object, they might spend all of their free time creating expressive residential architecture with skilled designers. But they continue to delight in their own house by refinishing woodwork, replanting gardens, and even rearranging the furniture. The success of the renovation has encouraged them to open the house to family and friends. And they are reminded daily that good craftsmanship as well as thoughtful design makes a house that evokes pleasure, even delight, long after it is finished.

Architects and Designers

Arkin Tilt Architects
1101 8th Street
Suite 180
Berkeley, CA 94710
(510) 528-9830
www.arkintilt.com
pp. 108–117

David Brown Architects
10613 S.W. 138th Street
Vashon Island, WA 98070
(206) 567 4410
pp. 188–197

Robert Cain, Architect
857 Vedado Way
Atlanta, GA 30308
(404) 892-8643
pp. 14–21

DWH Architects
405 Trujillo Lane
Taos, NM 87571
(505) 751-1479
pp. 130–139

Jeremiah Eck Architects
560 Harrison Avenue
Suite 403
Boston, MA 02118
(617) 367-9696
www.jearch.com
pp. 158–169

Estes/Twombly Architects
79 Thames Street
Newport, RI 02840
(401) 846-3336
www.estestwombly.com
pp. 40–51

HammerSmith
(Warner McConaughey)
807 Church Street
Decatur, GA 30030
(404) 377-1021
www.hammersmith.net
pp. 140–149

David Hertz Architects
2908 Colorado Avenue
Santa Monica, CA 90404
(310) 829-9932
www.syndesisinc.com
pp. 32–39

Lynn Hopkins
45 Munroe Road
Lexington, MA 02421
(781) 863-2585
pp. 78–87

Jacobson Silverstein Winslow
Architects
3106 Shattuck Avenue
Berkeley, CA 94705
(510) 848-8861
www.jswarch.com
pp. 52–59

Leger Wanaselja Architecture
2808 Adeline Street
Berkeley, CA 94703
(510) 848-8901
www.lwarch.com
pp. 170–179

Manning Architecture
365 Ericksen Avenue
Bainbridge Island, WA 98110
(206) 780-9026
pp. 60–69

McInturff Architects
4220 Leeward Place
Bethesda, MD 20816
(310) 229-3705
pp. 98–107

Mitchell Architecture
1324 East Green Meadow Lane
Greenwood Village CO 80121
(303) 795-8202
pp. 88–97

Moore Ruble Yudell
933 Pico Boulevard
Santa Monica, CA 90405
(310) 450-1400
www.moorerubleyudell.com
pp. 210–217

Prentiss Architects
224 West Galer
P.O. Box 955
Seattle, WA 98119
(206) 283-9930
www. prentissarch.com
pp. 180–187

Mark Sutherland
1640 West Hubbard
Chicago, IL 60622
(312) 492-9800
pp. 70–77

Swanston and Associates
801 South Dallas Street
Baltimore, MD 21231
(410) 732-0600
pp. 198–209

Dennis Wedlick Architect
85 Worth Street
New York, NY 10013
(212) 625-9222
www.dennis-wedlick.com
pp. 118–129

Lane Williams Architects
327 Second Avenue West
Seattle, WA 98119
(206) 284-8355
www.lanewilliams.com
pp. 150–157

Z:Architecture
(Matthew Schoenherr)
1052 Main Street
Suite 12 Branford, CT 06405
(203) 488-8484
pp. 22–31